SECULAR TRANSLATIONS

RUTH BENEDICT BOOK SERIES

RUTH BENEDICT BOOK SERIES

Edited by David Scott and Elizabeth A. Povinelli

Named after one of the founders of American anthropology and the Columbia Department of Anthropology, the Ruth Benedict Book Series is inspired by Benedict's passionate engagement with the critical political, aesthetic, and theoretical problems of the twentieth century but places them in the global conditions of the twenty-first. Contributions to the series explore contemporary critical thought in politics and aesthetics through a deep knowledge of the global condition in specific localities and regions. The scope of the series is capaciously theoretical and determinately international with special emphasis on settler-colonial, postcolonial, and capitalist regimes. The books present crisp interventions in a multiplicity of disciplines, but are also statements whose reckoning cuts across the critical humanistic and social sciences.

SECULAR TRANSLATIONS

NATION-STATE, MODERN SELF, AND CALCULATIVE REASON

TALAL ASAD

COLUMBIA UNIVERSITY PRESS   *New York*

COLUMBIA UNIVERSITY PRESS

Publishers Since 1893

New York   Chichester, West Sussex

cup.columbia.edu

Library of Congress Cataloging-in-Publication Data

Names: Asad, Talal, author.

Title: Secular translations : nation state, modern self, and calculative reason /
Talal Asad.

Description: New York : Columbia University Press, 2018. | Series: Ruth
Benedict book series | Includes bibliographical references and index.

Identifiers: LCCN 2018010138 | ISBN 9780231189866 (cloth : alk. paper) |
ISBN 9780231189873 (pbk. : alk. paper) | ISBN 9780231548595 (ebook)

Subjects: LCSH: Secularism. | Language and languages. | Reasoning. |
Secularization. | Religion and culture. | State, The.

Classification: LCC BL2747.8 .A755 2018 | DDC 306.6—dc23

LC record available at https://lccn.loc.gov/2018010138

Cover design: Chang Jae Lee

CONTENTS

ACKNOWLEDGMENTS

I thank Columbia University's Department of Anthropology for inviting me to deliver the first Ruth Benedict lectures in April 2017. I am particularly grateful to the following friends who read and commented on part of or the whole manuscript: Hussein Agrama, Gil Anidjar, Partha Chatterjee, Abou Farman, Charles Hirschkind, Mahmood Mamdani, David Scott, John Wallach.

SECULAR TRANSLATIONS

Introduction

This book is a slightly expanded version of the Ruth Benedict lectures I delivered to the Department of Anthropology at Columbia University in April 2017. It is an exploration, in the form of three interconnected essays, of a topic I have tried to think about for a number of years: the idea of the secular.

For me, the exploration of what language does *with* the subject (and not merely what the subject does *with* language), the attempt to discover how sentiments/concepts/attitudes articulate discourses in and about "the secular" and "the religious" in our contemporary life, has been best pursued through writing: through confronting the words one writes down, listening to them, being surprised—embarrassed or pleased. Anthropologists who encounter a very different form of life are familiar with this predicament, with trying to follow through and connect a welter of sometimes puzzling, sometimes familiar, experiences. Like ordinary life, exploration is partly a collective endeavor and its fruitfulness depends not only on interaction with the terrain but also on the knowledge of and cooperation with others. As patterns of ideas and arguments take shape (or change their shape), something that was unreachable becomes available. As with any exploration, thinking through writing means that one cannot know what lies ahead: One discovers thoughts, one doesn't create them. One isn't "free" in one's thinking. As an anthropologist, one can never separate oneself completely from the way of life one tries to understand—even although one pretends that this attachment is merely temporary, that as an objective scholar one can (and should) return from experience in the field as near as possible to an uninvolved point of view. But when one returns, one is often reminded of that time and place, of the possibility of another way of living and the necessity of writing about it.

Using a language, so Ludwig Wittgenstein proposed, is like playing a game, not like using a calculus. Understanding a language game is understanding a form of life. No appeal to rules guarantees that a statement has been uttered correctly, if only because it is possible to interpret and apply a rule incorrectly. To understand a way of life presupposes that one understands how its language is embedded in and articulates practices, that one can recognize a correct statement in a particular context, and that one can sometimes recognize different interpretations of that statement as obvious in a given situation. "You must bear in mind," Wittgenstein wrote, "that the language game is, so to speak, something unpredictable. I mean it is not based on grounds. It is not reasonable (or unreasonable). It is there—like our life."[1]

Understanding secularism, like understanding any dominant concept of modern life, is, I think, perhaps best approached indirectly. A straight line isn't always the most useful way to explore things because it assumes not only that the endpoint is known but also that the shortest way to it from the starting point is always the best. In this book I have therefore tried to move forward in an open, speculative way, recognizing that secularism is not only an abstract principle of equality and freedom that liberal democratic states are supposed to be committed to but also a range of sensibilities—ways of feeling, thinking, talking—that make opposites only by excluding affinities and overlaps. Perhaps the single most important sensibility is the *conviction* that one has a direct access to the "truth." Thus, when humanists conduct funeral rituals, they do so with the notable omission of any reference to God or to life after death, but the feeling that some pre-given formality is necessary appears to them to be a truth that is not in conflict with freedom. Taking an indirect approach is being aware that the object to be reached is not fully known.

So in the first chapter I think about some of the ambiguities in what is translated as "equality" in liberal state and society, a term crucial to secularism as a political ideology, and I address the claim that liberal equality is an inheritance from an earlier period of Christianity by considering some ideas about translation from religion to nonreligion. In the second chapter, I take up the question of untranslatability, and I analyze some aspects of translation into what some anthropologists have called the mindful body (but which I prefer to call the sensible body), by way of tradition and ritual that actuate the thoughts, behavior, and feelings of individuals. I insist that this translation does not hinge on the distinction between a real private self and a socially evident self, and I contrast this kind of translation with translation into numbers. In the third chapter, I explore ways in which the moral/political concept of a unique, self-governing agent (the so-called essential self) generates uncertainties in reading the intentions of the "real" self in relation to its public presentation, and the way statistical calculation comes to be regarded as an objective translation of social reality and a rational instrument for resolving future problems and eliminating obstacles inherited from the past.

What ties the three chapters together is therefore the idea of translation, because the transmission of ideas from the past and the inheritance of embodied practices, as well as uncertainties about the future, are of course all central to mutual understanding and interaction—although the sense of "translation" is not always the same in each instance of communication and action. Roman Jakobson has helpfully summed up different modes of translation in a well-known essay:

> For us, both as linguists and as ordinary word-users, the meaning of any linguistic sign is its translation into some further, alternative sign, especially a sign "in which it is more fully developed," as Peirce, the deepest inquirer into the essence of signs, insistently stated. The term "bachelor" may be converted into a more explicit designation, "unmarried man," whenever higher explicitness is required. We distinguish three ways of interpreting a verbal sign: it may be translated into other signs of the same language, into another language, or into another, nonverbal system of symbols. These three kinds of translation are to be differently labeled: 1) Intralingual translation or *rewording* is an interpretation of verbal signs by means of other signs of the same language. 2) Interlingual translation or *translation proper* is an interpretation of verbal sign by means of some other language. 3) Intersemiotic translation or *transmutation* is an interpretation of verbal signs by means of signs of nonverbal sign systems.[2]

The process of rewording and elaborating is part of every communication process. Jakobson's classification doesn't make quite explicit, however, that, for Peirce, every sign situation is a knowledge situation and that his epistemology replaces the dyadic relation between knowing mind and known fact characteristic of Cartesian philosophy with a triadic relation between sign, object signified, and interpretant.[3] Given that that is so, translation is never a direct move from discourse A to discourse B because it always involves an interpreting (mediating) sign X. That chain I see as the core of tradition, the move from one generation to another through translation, and through disputes over what is essential to the tradition, differences that must therefore be reflected in the translation. But there is this additional point: the sign as an object of a knowing mind (a purely cognitive event) is not the same as the sign translated into the sensible body through the cultivation of sensibilities.

I differ, therefore, from Jakobson's notion of "intersemiotic translation": in my view, while natural language is essential to the learning of embodied practices, the final result is not, strictly speaking, "an interpretation of verbal signs by signs of nonverbal sign systems." Cultivated practices of the self are *not* (necessarily) nonverbal sign systems—that is, carriers of meaning—although they can be meaningfully described as translations. They are, for the subject, ways of learning how to live in a given tradition. That is to say, discursive tradition is not merely a verbal process; it is also and primarily an implicit continuity embodied in habit, feeling, and behavior that one acquires as a member of a shared way of life that is translated from one time to another. So when speaking about disagreements over what constitutes the essence of the discursive tradition among its followers, one is concerned with the mode of reasoning and argument (using argument in the widest sense of a narrative or abstraction that seeks to inform) used to translate, affirm, or reject it. To enter debates about the tradition's essence is to enter, however briefly, the tradition—whether consciously or not. In other words, to claim to have identified a tradition's essence (whether structure or substance) is to try to persuade (or to dissuade) those who belong to the tradition to take up a particular position and inhabit a particular time.

Although in what follows I deal at first with what Jakobson calls "translation proper"—especially with Jürgen Habermas's proposal that religious language should be translated into secular if it is to qualify for the political sphere—I go on to suggest that when verbal models are used to discipline the religious body (or techniques used to write and play a piece of music) they are not strictly speaking *replaced* by nonverbal sign systems because signs as signs gradually disappear into *the way* a particular life is expressed and lived. As Wittgenstein puts it, life is just there. However, there *is* a form of translation from verbal signs belonging to a natural language to a unique (abstractive and universal) language, the language of mathematics, a language to which I return at the very end of the book.

The translation of values from one natural language to another is always problematic, as every anthropologist who has carried out research in a society that speaks a language foreign to her own knows. Which is why what makes sense to a Western ethnographer in a nonmodern community sometimes doesn't do so as easily when she returns home to Euro-America. It is almost impossible to abstract an important idea that indicates something distinctive of a particular form of life and find a ready word in a language belonging to a very different form of life for reasons that I try to explore.

Every translation from one natural language to another—or even *within* one language—is, in ways both trivial and profound, also a transformation. Jakobson insists that "all cognitive experience and its classification is conveyable in any existing language. Whenever there is deficiency, terminology may be qualified and amplified by loanwords or loan-translations, neologisms or semantic shifts, and finally, by circumlocutions."[4] And yet, arguably, translation (indeed, every use of language in what Wittgenstein called a language game) is not a *purely* cognitive enterprise—in which signifying words can be substituted for others—but a complex of expressions that evoke, in particular contexts, particular sounds, images, and feelings in what is rendered and that help to realize actions and attitudes. Jakobson concedes as much by saying that in translating *poetry*, "Only creative transposition is possible: either intralingual transposition—from one poetic shape into another, or interlingual transposition—from one language into another, or finally intersemiotic transposition—from one system of signs into another, e.g., from verbal art into music, dance, cinema, or painting."[5] I have already indicated my reservation about this way of formulating the *entire* idea of translation. But one should ask: What exactly is "poetry" that it resists a standard conceptualization of translation? Jakobson's article ends perceptively: "If we were to translate into English the traditional formula *Tradutore, traditore* as 'the translator is a betrayer,' we would deprive the Italian rhyming epigram of all its paronomastic value. Hence a cognitive attitude would compel us to change this aphorism into a more explicit statement and to answer the questions: translator of what messages? betrayer of what values?"[6] So one might say that poetry is what alerts us to the fact that in any translation a particular message is selected and some values are dismissed. But the process of selection is not solely cognitive; it depends on sensibilities that are the products of shifting experiences of the sensible body. The question of poetry, of what is selected and what is forgotten and what is impossible to translate, is intrinsic to every act of narrative re-presentation—including nationalist stories.

In his introduction to David Ferry's remarkable translation of the great Babylonian epic *Gilgamesh*—from which I cite some lines in my epilogue—William Moran writes that "[Ferry] has given us, not a translation, not at least as that term is ordinarily understood, but a transformation. . . . He has given us what [earlier translators] have not and what as authors of word-for-word translations they could not aspire to. He has given us a work of verbal art. He has thereby communicated to us some sense of the beauty of the original and some sense of the emotions that reading or hearing the original must have aroused."[7] Whether the feelings evoked in our reading are those of listeners four thousand years ago is, of course, impossible to ascertain. So perhaps it would be more acceptable to say that Ferry's translation reflects part of the *potential* of the original, but that his translation is (as Ferry himself describes it) a "rendering" in English expressing *our* view of the world, especially our notion of an archaic world. His purpose is not, so it could be argued, to re-evoke the original experience of the epic's audience in Babylon but to reproduce its ritual character, its sense of irreducible powers, for English readers today and thus to contribute to an understanding of formal tradition. Hence, the formal repetition of utterances in the rendering that describe and recapitulate events—both triumphant and disastrous—in the epic. Its potential resides in the possibility that the hearer may transcend a purely cognitive approach (the assumption that a story in one language can be satisfactorily translated into words from another) by confronting the secular sense that the essence of being human is the freedom to approach an ancient text as one wishes.

"Translatability is an essential quality of certain works," writes Walter Benjamin,

> which is not to say that it is essential that they be translated; it means rather that a specific significance inherent in the original manifests itself in its translatability. It is plausible that no translation, however good it may be, can have any significance as regards the original. Yet, by virtue of its translatability the original is closely connected with the translation; in fact, this connection is all the closer since it is no longer of importance to the original. We may call this connection a natural one, or, more specifically, a vital connection. Just as the manifestations of life are intimately connected with the phenomenon of life without being of importance to it, a translation issues from the original—not so much from its life as from its afterlife.[8]

Translatability is, of course, always a matter of *what* can be translated and how. Benjamin refers to translation from and into natural languages. But when translation of words into numbers takes place, there is also something essential that is discarded so that it belongs only to the afterlife of the original, creating new possibilities and new dangers.

It is not an incidental fact that anthropologists consider fieldwork (living another form of life in order to learn about it) essential for understanding what people in another society typically do, say, and feel—and why some things and not others seem right there but not here. This anthropological experience is a unique and perhaps inadequately appreciated way of understanding. However, it may be noted that very few anthropologists "go native" because (so I have heard it said) our deepest feelings are truly at home only in our own time and our own society. And yet: innumerable immigrants from the South have entered Euro-America to live in and learn about another form of life they look to as their future. But the reverse is not true. For when Europeans went to the South, it was as conquerors and missionaries—or, in the so-called New World, as colonial settlers displacing indigenous societies. Asymmetries of power, in other words, continue to define ways of understanding as well as projects for the future. And one aspect of this is still not as clearly grasped by many anthropologists: it is one thing to try to understand "the native's point of view," as Bronislaw Malinowski urged ethnographers to do in his introduction to *Argonauts of the Pacific*;[9] it is quite another for the anthropologist to approach "the native" with the possibility of learning something important for her own form of life that might help to transform how that life is understood. Attention to "the native's point of view" as such is, after all, compatible with an entirely instrumental approach—with viewing the native's form of life simply as information to be translated for a purpose entirely foreign to it.

"Poetry," etymologically, has to do with "making." Taking up this meaning, I emphasize the *denial* of a certain potentiality in the political translation advocated by theorists like Jürgen Habermas. Unlike Walter Benjamin, Habermas does not regard translation as a challenge to expand the receiving language and way of life. (A challenge does not mean that one must accept the challenger's argument but that one must respond in an appropriate sense.) When I discuss the remaking of body and soul, I contrast it with the translation of political information enabled by the use of numbers to make and remake life collectively; these two kinds of translation are, I suggest, mutually antagonistic kinds of *poiesis*. In the modern state and modern market, abstraction and generalization enable practical collections of "the same" to be used for specific purposes of governing subjects that modern morality regards as unique. But the use of mathematical language goes well beyond the immediate interests of political control and commercial profit: it is central to the inventiveness and future orientation found in developments such as artificial intelligence and genetic engineering. As such these secular developments are a source of understandable concern.

The astonishing achievements of modern science, technology, and industry, so I maintain finally, not only mark the triumph of mathematical calculation and secular reason; they also point to a dark future: the certainty of climate change and environmental destruction and the probability of nuclear war. I find it a remarkable irony, incidentally, that up to about the end of the Second World War, if not later, European (or Christian) civilization was triumphantly declared to be the creator of the modern world but that now, confronted with a menacing future, it is more common to hear people talk about *humanity's* self-destruction—as though the peasants and working classes of the world had the same responsibility for that future as the industrialists, politicians, military careerists, bankers, and arms manufacturers. My point, however, is not to identify who is to blame ("modernity," "European civilization," "humanity") but to stress the obvious need to identify the languages and forms of life that may lead us into disaster.

I end with a memorable passage from Daniel Ellsberg's latest book because it is about a condition that overshadows all our lives:

> In sum, most aspects of the U.S. nuclear planning system and force readiness that became known to me half a century ago still exist today, as prone to catastrophe as ever but on a scale, as now known to environmentalist scientists, looming vastly larger than was understood then. The present risks of the current nuclear era go far beyond the dangers of proliferation and non-state terrorism that have been the almost exclusive focus of public concern for the past generation and the past decade in particular. The arsenals and plans of the two super-powers represent not only an insuperable obstacle to an effective global anti-proliferation campaign; they are in them-selves a clear and present existential danger to the human species, and most others. . . . No policies in human history have more deserved to be recognized as immoral. Or insane. The story of how this calamitous predicament came about and how and why it has persisted for over half a century is a chron-icle of human madness. Whether Americans, Russians, and other humans can rise to the challenge of reversing these pol-icies and eliminating the danger of near-term extinction caused by their own inventions and proclivities remains to be seen. I choose to join others in acting *as if* that is still possible.[10]

Of course, human beings are as capable of compassionate behavior as of cruelty and selfishness. The horror that threatens is not essen-tially a matter of "human nature" but of ambivalences and grid-locks that exist in our collective form of life.

Every adult is familiar with the fragility and finitude of individual life, but the elimination of virtually all life from our earth is—emotionally and cognitively—an ungraspable idea. Which is why, understandably, most of us prefer not to think of it. In the brief explorations that follow, I proceed in the unreasonable hope that a human future is possible—and that anthropology, as a modern discipline, has a small part in keeping that hope alive.

1

Secular Equality and Religious Language

I

In a recent article on the demographic danger of Muslim immigrants in Europe to what he calls "liberal moral values," the British economist and politician Lord Robert Skidelsky cites the political philosopher Larry Siedentop as saying "secularization is Christianity's gift to the world."[1] Siedentop puts the matter this way:

What is the crux of secularism? It is that belief in an underlying or moral equality of humans implies that there is a sphere in which each should be free to make his or her own decisions, a sphere of conscience and free action. That belief is summarized in the central value of classical liberalism: the commitment to "equal liberty." Is this indifference or non-belief? Not at all. It rests on the firm belief that to be human means being a rational and moral agent, a free chooser with responsibility for one's actions. It puts a premium on conscience rather than the "blind" following of rules. It joins rights with duties to others. This is also the central egalitarian moral insight of Christianity. It stands out from

St Paul's contrast between "Christian liberty" and observance of the Jewish law.[2]

Christianity, Siedentop tells us, is connected to its secular successor by the values of equality, freedom of choice, and conscience—
values that in different ways also underlie the rise of liberal society.
Skidelsky and Siedentop are not the first to claim that Christianity and secularism are intimately related, although the political moment in which they do so is significant. Several major European writers have made that claim—including Max Weber, Carl
Schmitt, Karl Löwith, Matthew Arnold, and Ernest Renan.

This view of the Christian origins of secularism, of secular ideas
as a modern translation of Christianity, has been contested by those
who argue that secularization has its own genealogy, one that represents a profound break from religion and enchantment—a break
that is marked by the emergence of modern science and modern
politics. I'll turn briefly to this debate in a moment, but first I want
to pose a question. Why is it important for self-described secularists to claim a Christian heritage? Personal motives are obviously
difficult to establish at this level, but one can clearly see what the
effect of such a claim is: the political exclusion of all those who cannot claim that heritage. What proponents of this thesis mean when
they refer to Christianity is, of course, European Christianity,
which, in the early encounter of Europeans with non-Europeans
(especially with the construction of European empires dominating
non-Europeans), became an important part of their identity. There
were of course forms of Christianity in Eastern Europe, Northeast
Africa, and West Asia, but these were dismissed as irrational or
decadent forms of essential Christianity. The redefinition of the
heritage from which Europe claims to derive secularity as *Judeo-*
Christian comes at the end of a long history of Christian ambivalence toward Jews, ending with the Nazi Holocaust; the new term
is, like so many other connected moves, designed to be taken as a

sign of genuine repentance and reconciliation, but it is a Christian perspective on the outmoded place of the Jews in theological history.[3] The claim to a Judeo-Christian heritage is now invoked by secularists in the European Union as a grammatical exclusion of Muslims.

A famous moment in this debate is Max Weber's *The Protestant Ethic and the Spirit of Capitalism*, which paradoxically suggests that an aspect of Protestant behavior (morality) is translated into the god of capitalist society (accumulation). Less well known are his comments in "Science as a Vocation," where he writes of secularization as consisting of disenchantment through intellectualization and rationalization. This process consists, he argues, not of increased knowledge in which the modern individual lives, but in

> the knowledge or belief that if one but wished one *could* learn it at any time. Hence, it means that principally there are no mysterious incalculable forces that come into play, but rather that one can, in principle, master all things by calculation. This means that the world is disenchanted. One need no longer have recourse to magical means in order to master or implore the spirits, as did the savage, for whom such mysterious powers existed. Technical means and calculations perform the service. This above all is what intellectualization means.[4]

The secular as disenchantment is not to be seen simply as part of the move toward religious separation from political authority but as a vision of rational and therefore justified hierarchy.

Fifty years ago, Hans Blumenberg defended what he and other German writers called "the self-assertion" of the modern world (its scientific knowledge, democratic politics, and individualist morality) brought about by secularization (*Verweltlichung*). This secular response, he argued, was not simply the recovery of "worldliness"—of a reality that is assumed to have been always there even while it was obscured by medieval (i.e., mythical) beliefs about God as the supreme governor of nature—but of something more complex.[5] That is to say, when beliefs about divine omnipotence are abandoned, one is not necessarily left with Christian ideas that can be used for nonreligious purposes: "As soon as one leaves the sphere of influence of the theological system of categories," Blumenberg writes, "the world to which the modern age appears to have turned its full attention can be an 'unworldly' world in regard to its concept of reality or to the nature of its intuition as compared to an immediacy ascribed to the ancients."[6] In other words, secularization doesn't merely enable human beings to see the world as it really is; it does this by establishing a distance between self and external reality, something that primitives (so Europeans believed) can't do. One result of this separation, according to Blumenberg, is the sense of loss and pessimism about the advent of modernity found in Romanticism.

The claim that the central values of "classical liberalism" (and of secularization) are translated from Christian history doesn't attend to the fact that what is now taken to be "equality" and what was identified as such in medieval Christendom actually differ profoundly. Thus, when Jürgen Habermas argues that the Christian concept of *imago Dei*, "Man created in the image of God," can be translated into the political demand that all human beings be treated equally, he ignores a semantic rupture.[7] In order for the idea of man created in the image of God to be given a worldly sense, it must first be purged of the belief (much emphasized by Protestant theologians) that the Fall, leading to Adam's expulsion from Eden into the world, rendered man corrupt—and therefore redeemable only by divine grace. That idea must then be put into a context in which rights and dignity are assumed to be universal and unconditional—an a priori assumption with *no* connection whatever to otherworldliness or divine grace. *That* sense of a "secular" world is incomprehensible to medieval Christians, who needed to be justified in the world by a theology of grace that is, in turn, incomprehensible to secular moderns.

I want to begin with the various interpretations (translations) of equality in the secular state because it is arguably the most important value not only for political secularism (as the principle of government neutrality) but for liberalism too (the right of everyone to believe and practice freely, and so to refuse to practice any religion). The idea of freedom is at least as important as equality for classical liberalism, but precisely because it is *equal* freedom that is valued— equal freedom for all individual citizens. That is precisely why Siedentop speaks of "equal liberty." Over and beyond that, there must be equal opportunity for all, equal treatment for everyone who appears before the law, equal respect for all human beings, and equal participation of all citizens (religious or secular) in politics. All these instances of equality are articulated within and by the liberal democratic state.

The principle of equality is the subject of a vast philosophical literature. Perhaps the most widely debated work in recent political theory is that of John Rawls, beginning with *A Theory of Justice* and ending with *Justice as Fairness: A Restatement*. His claim to being a liberal theorist derives from the overriding priority he gives to liberty at the expense of equality. He does this by distinguishing between two principles: "the first principle" (equal basic freedoms for all citizens) and "the second principle" (fair equality of opportunity) by which inequalities are countenanced on condition that economic and social inequalities benefit the least well off in society according to what is known as "the difference principle." But who decides that the least well off are optimally benefited by a particular structure of inequality, and by what criteria, is highly ambiguous to say the least. The role of translation in elaborating these principles is clearly central. Thus, when the founders of the American Republic, who are a major part of the story of liberalism, attached liberty not to politics but to property, they enabled some citizens to recognize and accept one another as unequal, but the initial separation between economic and political equality is not in itself unproblematic. Whether the inequality is meant to reflect what the rich deserve (they are more talented than the unsuccessful) or what they need (they have more expenses than the poor) is not easy to establish "rationally."

Like liberty, equality is evidently an ambiguous notion recognized in different, often contradictory ways. Its attraction consists in what it opens up as well as in what it hides. But it is also feared because the pursuit of equality unleashes threats: "populism," "irrationality," "intolerance," and the refusal to recognize "talent and innovation." Enshrined in secularization, the political origins and consequences of equality are often unexpected and contrary to what its liberal supporters would want to be the case. Secularization, in other words, doesn't simply transform the general understanding of religion; it also—and more significantly—transforms the idea of politics that is framed by the sovereign state's claim to be based on territorial exclusivity and equally distributed rights.

Sovereignty is itself part of the emerging language of liberalism, part of a claim to the self-generation of political power, of a claim to the right and possibility of gathering and exercising an exclusive, coercive power within state territory.[8] But in a world of global capitalism in which corporations help shape policies and politics, this claim is as utopian as any anarchist rejection of all centralized, coercive power. Liberal democracy accepts centralized state power and yet distrusts it (hence "minimal government") and at the same time distrusts the coercive power of the energized demos (hence the need to control "the people's worst instincts"). Secularism is one way—in theory, at least—of dealing with this problem: it denies the right of "religion" to legitimize overwhelming state power, and it represses "religious passions" among the people that can only generate intolerance and disruption.

II

I have cited authors who take secularism and liberalism to be closely linked together. I am particularly interested here in the way liberal language has been invoked to affirm a variety of principles regarded as central to secularism, including, most importantly, the interconnected principles of freedom, equality, and neutrality. Neutrality on the part of the state, it should be noted, presupposes equality between two options, and equality implies the right of each individual to act autonomously. However, when attempts are made to systematize that language in the messiness of ordinary life, the results are often contradictory—so that neutrality, for example, comes to underwrite inequality.[9]

Of course, secularization has been undertaken not only by liberal democratic states but by authoritarian states, too, and this only shows how ambiguous liberal language is, how committed both types of secular state are, above all, to the definition and maintenance of modern power. It is this ambiguity (sometimes called "richness") that makes it possible for one writer to present Karl Marx and John Stuart Mill as at once sharply contrasting thinkers and yet partly in agreement about visions of liberty, and for another to describe the slave-holding political elite of Revolutionary America as integral to the history of liberalism.[10]

One might put the matter this way: historically, secularism has framed the modern state in different ways, but it is sustained by typical feelings and beliefs about reasonableness, equality, and freedom that are themselves ambiguous. The secular individual thinks of herself as autonomous and rational—even when she can choose a form of life she regards as "real religion." But what autonomy and rationality mean are not always clear, and even when they are, they are not historically constant. Ideologically, freedom of choice and freedom of speech are said to be foundational rights of individuals in a liberal (and secular) society and state—the choice of what to do, what to consume, what to believe and what to say.[11] The story is that it is precisely the differentiation of social institutions and domains that becomes part of the condition allowing citizens to make choices freely—especially between religions as well as between "religion" and "no-religion"—and thereby to affirm the autonomy of all individual identities.[12]

Of course, not all versions of liberalism are identical, and so secularization follows different paths according to different historical circumstances. When liberalism is motivated by the principle of neutrality, its secularism endorses pluralism even when that is difficult to reconcile with equality; when it is motivated by tolerance, it remains committed to converting the world to "civilization" and thus to a *particular* form of class and race entitlement. Liberalism has a shifting historical identity. It has changed from being a revolutionary movement in the seventeenth and eighteenth centuries (when it aimed to circumscribe the privileges of church and monarch) to being socially conservative in the nineteenth and twentieth centuries (when it sought to consolidate elite power and imperial advantage) and, most recently, to being predatory (when it not only accelerated market freedoms but also encouraged the global dominance of finance capital and promoted the growth of inequality).[13] It is the insistence on telling a single, coherent story that allows one to pretend that these radical differences are moments in the historical life of liberalism. Whether and to what extent liberalism remains "the same" depends on the way state law and politics—and the collective experience and memory of particular groups of citizens—interpret liberty and threats to liberty. The sensibilities of eighteenth- and nineteenth-century liberals are not those of liberals in the twentieth and twenty-first century. Like all great historical ideologies, liberal language contains the possibility of insight and self-deception, compassion and ruthlessness. There is no "real liberalism," although in everyday life people speak meaningfully of "liberal" and "illiberal" actions, and of liberal democracy as a political system, to celebrate or condemn particular attitudes and ideas because that is how the terms have been learned and used.

Thus, in late-nineteenth-century Britain, many feared that the extension of the suffrage would lead to the dispossession of the wealthy, that a flourishing capitalism and mass democracy were incompatible. But the ideological separation of economic inequality from political equality proved an effective defense of privilege. After the Second World War, liberalism, capitalism, and democracy became indissolubly bound together. It was and is widely assumed by liberals that the welfare state moderated the excesses of capitalism and that any radical rearrangement of the property system would be unacceptable to most citizens not only because of its threat to their civil, social, and political rights but also to their personal identities. However, the welfare state that most liberals regard as a triumph of compassion and moral progress is seen by many socialists and anarchists as binding the mass of citizens to the state by shifting a significant part of their income from waged labor to state benefits in the form of education, old-age pension, and health care, and thus to dependence on bourgeois inequality.

In *The Liberal Tradition in America*, Louis Hartz argues the reason there has never been a Liberal Party or a Socialist one in America is that, unlike Europe, its liberalism did not need to destroy a feudal structure in order to establish a democracy and that, because America never experienced feudalism (although the pre–Civil War South fantasized that its society was feudal), American liberalism is unique. The book's thesis is encapsulated in its epigraph, a famous quotation from Alexis de Tocqueville: "The great advantage of the Americans is, that they have arrived at a state of democracy without having to endure a democratic revolution; and that they are born equal, instead of becoming so." But Hartz does not really examine the implications for liberalism of the structured inequality of slavery and of ethnic massacre and expulsion as the frontier expanded and land was freed for a population of European origin.[14]

In other words, liberal democracy and secularism are *together* rooted in—even constitutive of—the modern liberal state.[15] As such, the common assumption that secularism prescribes the separation of religion and state and upholds equality and freedom is perhaps better reformulated as follows: secularism and liberal democracy were centrally involved in *linking* religion to the nation, attaining civil rights for citizens (especially social and political equality), and thus forming the liberal democratic state as a power state. It is worth recalling here that it was Thomas Hobbes who first made the classic argument connecting what we now think of as civil rights (the freedom, equality, etc., of subjects/citizens) with authoritarian acts of the sovereign state necessary for securing its power both within and beyond its territory. In this sense Hobbes demonstrates the necessity of having to balance what we would today call liberal and authoritarian tendencies of the state. For after all, while liberalism ideologically distrusts strong government, it requires that government be strong enough to protect religious freedom and control religious passions—each task requiring considerable social power.

One of the most important liberal values is, of course, free speech—that is to say, unconstrained speech held as a right by everyone even though the exercise of this right by some secularists sometimes offends the religious sensibilities of others. The political philosopher Glen Newey has argued that, in spite of the very different kinds of formal and informal limitation to which speech in society is actually subject, what makes it plausible to treat the idea of free speech as a single absolute right held equally by every citizen is the assumption that it is essential to *free association*, another basic right vested equally in all citizens.[16] Thus, in the various spheres of communicative exchange (clubs, theaters, parliament, lecture halls, etc.), there are rules that limit speech in ways that help to define what the point of those spaces is. The people who enter these defined social spaces do so voluntarily—thereby indicating their agreement to the specific limits to communication within the institutionalized spaces they choose to enter. So his argument is that the real concern of free speech advocates is the equal right of everyone to *freedom of association*: because the generic purpose of speech is communication, limits to free speech become obstacles to free association, historically promoted by secularism. This makes much sense, but what Newey doesn't address are the restrictions to communication put in place by the state (such as leaking "state secrets") and the state's duty to punish its citizens for treason. Is citizenship really based on free choice, rendering the individual subject to the authority and law of the state? This would be how contractual theorists of political obligation (whose real concern is to find ways of postulating state legitimacy) see it, but the reality seems to indicate otherwise: African Americans did not choose to come to North America (except very recently), nor were Native Americans voluntary members of the order established internally by the United States. Equally important for this argument, most people are born citizens within the territory of particular states and did not choose to become their citizens.

In his vigorous defense of the modern state and modern politics, Pierre Manent makes the familiar contrast between the old political order, founded on command–obedience, and modern liberal democracy resting on institutionalized differences: the distancing of church from state, the division of labor, the separation of powers, the distinction of representatives from those represented. "One might say," Manent observes, "that I command myself through the intermediary of the government. In the end, I obey only myself."[17] This echoes Jean-Jacques Rousseau's conclusion to his account of the civil state—that is, of the status of the citizen: "We might, over and above all this, add, to what man acquires in the civil state, moral liberty, which alone makes him truly master of himself; for the mere impulse of appetite is slavery, while obedience to a law which we prescribe to ourselves is liberty."[18]

My first thought on reading Manent's echo of Rousseau (and Immanuel Kant) was that the subject considered at once as ruler-and-ruled, as entitled to command and required to obey, may indicate a form of psychosis: when government surveillance invades the private lives of citizens and controls the way they can speak, act, and think, the subjects believe they are controlling and protecting themselves. This belief, I will argue later, becomes the pivot of a pathological politics.

The liberal drive that helped produce separation and equality has continued relentlessly, a result that Manent celebrates as follows:

> There is no leaving behind the individualistic order and even the bourgeois order. Everyone is seen as an owner whose property the state and society must respect, but the property no longer consists only of goods, even including, as does Locke, life and liberty. It consists also of opinions, "values," "identities," and "orientations." I am the legitimate owner of all that I am. The state and society must recognize and declare that. They must explicitly approve all that I am.[19]

But since the identity of the state is also, as Manent earlier argued, my identity, I know that what the state orders is what I must do. In liberal democratic society, the philosophical sense of "property" (the essential character of something) is translated into the economic sense of "ownership" (disposable rights in things), thus giving wealth a fundamental role in the direction of policy.

Like all ideologies, liberal secularism has been shaped by its historical context, by the form of life its vocabulary feeds on and encourages. For those seeking to understand liberalism, it is crucial to ask precisely what kind of freedom and equality are being advocated, by whom they are resisted, and *how* they are conceded.

It is in the processes of ongoing social activity that the terms "liberalism," "secularity," and "religion" are used and contested. Precisely because language is interwoven with practice, a usage that makes sense in a given form of life may cease to do so when that life changes—translation is therefore a continuous and necessary feature of everyday life. Secularization may be seen as the fundamental change in the grammar of "religion," and of its associated vocabulary. I will argue later that secularization is always in tension, in different ways, with what may be called "ritualization."

In brief, the Enlightenment story of "secularism" replacing "religion" even as clarity replaces confusion, and as tolerance replaces bigotry, is unpersuasive. Not only have secular sensibility, belief, and agency evolved in interaction with elements of religion that secularism has defined itself against (and appropriated through translation as "superior truth"); the claims of secular persons to certainty have also been as marked as those of religious persons—if not often more so.[20]

III

The principle of *legal equality*, the main form in which equality is authorized in the liberal democratic state, accords each citizen the same legal rights (the right to vote, the right to a fair trial, etc.) and obligations as every other. All citizens, so the principle goes, are equally protected by the law and equally obligated to obey the law. However, everyone who appears before the law is to be judged in the same way as every other, with the understanding that every fact relevant to the case in hand is taken into account. Thus, where race and religious background are *irrelevant*, it is attention to these factors that demonstrates what is wrong and not the violation of equality as a universal norm. It is not a case of the need to treat people equally but of treating them wrongly—that is, by reference to criteria that are not relevant to the matter in hand. This is precisely what justifies the principle of affirmative action: that an attempt is being made to right a historical wrong.

The abstract notion of equality has unexpected consequences: Where two individuals are considered absolutely equal (as abstract categories), the choice by bureaucrats of one or the other should be a matter of indifference. In other words, when faced with *equals* (substitutables) from among whom he chooses, an official may do so without it being obviously invidious. But faced with what the law says are absolute equals, he may still choose on precisely that basis: a Muslim over a Copt in Egypt, a Jew over a Palestinian in Israel, a non-Muslim over a Muslim in France, a white over a black in the United States. It is often difficult for others (or for himself, for that matter) to recognize that a wrongful choice is being made, or for anyone else to prove wrongful discrimination. Only a statistical analysis of a collection of choices indicates individual choices as wrongful because it defines the bias. Or more properly: only an analysis of large numbers reveals the "truth" of social reality. That pattern shows that an unjustifiable selection (i.e., *not* based on merit but on sentiment) is being made—the injustice being not the unequal treatment of *one* candidate but of bias in favor of a candidate belonging to a category irrelevant to the official criteria of the position for which the choice is being made, and therefore a deviation from the norm that citizens must not be treated wrongly where being treated wrongly means being treated according to irrelevant criteria.

Incidentally, when "equality of opportunity" was first used in 1891, it simply meant the right to employment without discrimination—that is, the right to be considered eligible for employment solely on the basis of one's expertise.[21] In liberal secular societies, it has come to mean rather loosely as *the* drive for "equality." In practice, the term now refers to the right to compete on equal terms—a right that, as I argue later, promotes a careerist morality that is in conflict with a democratic ethos (although not with a democratic state). At any rate, to the extent that the principle of equality means "treating people who are in the same situation in the same way," it is a normatively vacuous tautology.[22]

Particular circumstances, including individual responsibility and injury to others, the kind of expertise sought, and a candidate's experience as well as laws passed for particular reasons, are all part of what is relevant to the judgment. Legal equality is not a universal yardstick but something that is finally vindicated at the conclusion of contested cases. It is not simply the allegation that a violation of a general legal rule has occurred but the claim that a particular injustice has been done and so calls for rectification. This claim is argued in a particular language by reference to particular facts—legal facts and facts relevant to the law—that are embedded in a particular form of life. The normativity in everyday life (whether explicit or implicit) proceeds in a similar fashion even in the absence of institutionalized judgment.

There are thus many questions for understanding the political thrust of equality, as I indicated earlier. Central to the debate about whether and, if so, to what extent it should be instituted revolves around how moral and practical "relevance" is to be defined. But the primary concern seems to be about actual or potential injustice. When workers go on strike for the right to unionize (self-defense) and for better working conditions (humane treatment), they are not asking for equality with managers (still less for equality with workers in poorer countries) but for justice. If a black person in America is entitled to "equality," it is not because a white person has been treated in a certain way. The movement calling itself "Black Lives Matter" is not translatable into "All Lives Matter" because it expresses a strong sense of wrong suffered by blacks precisely because they are black—wrongs that the movement demands must be put right. In this, it does not aspire to equality with whites (something that liberals might argue for) but with the correction of an injustice—even if that justice is not achievable in the present structure of powers and interests.

IV

So what do liberals understand equality to be in the secular nation-state? The influential jurist Ronald Dworkin maintains that all liberal political values can be seen as aspects of equality. "What does it mean for the government to treat its citizens as equals?" he asks.

> That is, I think, the same question as the question of what it means for the government to treat all its citizens as free, or as independent, or with equal dignity. . . . It may be answered in two fundamentally different ways. The first supposes that government must be neutral on what may be called the question of the good life. The second supposes that government cannot be neutral on that question, because it cannot treat its citizens as equal human beings without a theory of what human beings ought to be like.[23]

He then proceeds to argue that it is the first conception of equality that is constitutive of liberal political morality.

According to Ira Katznelson, who cites Dworkin in agreement on this matter, the liberal meaning of equality is " 'the requirement that the government treat all those in its charge *as equals*,' that is, with feelings of concern and respect."[24] This emphasis on treating each person with "concern and respect" reflects the new prominence given to the translation of "property" as an essential dimension of individual identity that Manent noted, because treating someone with concern and respect presupposes a recognition of that person's being an owner of who and what they are—their "identity." Although "identity" is regarded as something that is at last given its due in liberal society, it is worth noting that this modern notion has become a prominent part of public discourse only since the end of the Second World War as a result of the influence on public discourse of psychoanalysis and the social sciences, and of political concern with "ethnicity" from which individuals allegedly derive their "identity," because of the so-called identity crises.[25]

But there is more here than the claim of individual identity; it also stipulates an obligation on the part of government officials. And yet the equal treatment of citizens by state bureaucrats must be expressed (so it is often insisted) in indifference—that is to say, *without* feelings of personal concern that might favor one person's circumstance against another's.[26] In other words, each person is to be regarded abstractly as a citizen and, in that capacity, as substitutable for any other. To the extent that the liberal idea of equal respect works (as in respect for universal rights), it is clearly different from the thick sense of *solicitous concern* that Dworkin and Katznelson seem to have in mind (respect for a human life in a particular predicament). In brief, where equality requires *indifference* toward large numbers of people—as in the treatment of patients in a hospital, say, or of passengers traveling by train—it can lead to the authoritative application of an abstract rule about things or to what some complain of as "inhumane treatment."

On the other hand, sentiments of respect alleged to be distinctive of the liberal bureaucrat are in fact found in the politics of many preliberal societies. Thus, in a famous essay, J. G. A. Pocock once described the place that concern and respect had in eighteenth-century Anglo-America: deference, in that hierarchical society, was at once a political relationship and a personal style, a recognition that one had to negotiate differential social capabilities and political powers. In that world, "deference" and "influence" were distinguished such that it was the patron's "influence" rather than

the client's "deference" that afforded the former's means of manipu-
lating the latter. Nevertheless, influence and deference were ambig-
uously interconnected: "Deference was not merely [the client's]
means of inducing the patron to grant what he had to offer, but
also the means of reminding the patron that it was not his business
to reduce the client to dependence in the sense of *servility*, but to
treat him in a way which acknowledged the independence and
self-respect of both parties."[27] Both parties, says Pocock, were thus
bound by a code of formal behavior ("ritualization") by which the
spontaneous expression of immediate feelings was kept under
control—except in circumstances where the arrogance of the patron
might be responded to with self-respecting anger. In the eighteenth
century, the British state was not yet recognizably secular (although
it is argued that the American Constitution, by virtue of its dises-
tablishment of religion, was), but in both Britain and America the
tradition of deference went together with a sense of mutual concern and respect as expressed in formalities. This is not to say, of
course, that that ideal was always realized. It is simply that the formal inequality articulated by deference was an acceptable style in
evident contrast with the formal right to equality and freedom held
by individuals in a modern liberal state. Or was it?

Albert Hirschman has emphasized that deference is essential for
a secular representative democracy. Summing up a line of public
reasoning, he notes: "on the one hand, the citizen must express his
point of view so that the political elites know and can be responsive to what he wants, but, on the other, these elites must be allowed
to make decisions. The citizen must thus be in turn influential and
deferential."[28] It has been increasingly recognized—and to some
degree theorized—that the citizen's influence on her government
is highly limited at the best of times. There are important differences, of course, between the system of political patronage in
eighteenth-century European states and modern liberal democracy,
not least in the legal prohibition of slavery and the ending of legal

discrimination against women. It may be argued, however, that most differences are essentially matters of style: there are certainly different investments of emotion, different uses of theological language, different moral vocabularies—as well as different forms of exploitation and corruption. But Hirschman stresses the elite's freedom to make political decisions and exercise social control both in the state and in civil society—indicating thus the privileges of power in liberal democratic society. There is now certainly a new story according to which particular forms of inequality (religious, legal, etc.) are definitively replaced by equality. To the extent that unequal wealth and power are not regarded as critical, what this discourse of equality seeks is not the elimination of hierarchy but its invisibility.

The main point I want to stress here is that simply counterposing "subordination" to "equality" may not be an adequate way of understanding the deep character of political relations in modern society because the very concept of "politics"—its scope and content—has shifted significantly over time and space.

V

But there are other entanglements of the idea of equal concern and respect for all individuals with forms of inequality in the process of secularization—the language of human rights being perhaps the most notable. Those who regard secularism as an integral part of liberalism insist that its central virtue is the treatment of *all* persons, not only citizens, with equal concern and respect. In this context Article 1 of the Universal Declaration of Human Rights is often invoked: "All human beings are born free and equal in dignity and rights." Article 10(i) of the International Covenant on Civil and Political Rights is more specific: "All persons deprived of their liberty shall be treated with humanity and with respect for the inherent dignity of the human person." Such statements are some-times traced back to the Declaration of the Rights of Man and of the Citizen at the end of the eighteenth century, whose Article 6 declares that "all citizens being equal in the eyes of the law, are equally eligible to all dignities and to all public positions and occu-pations, according to their abilities and without distinction except that of their virtues and talents." However, Samuel Moyn has made the persuasive argument that the emergence of human rights dis-course is more recent than the French Revolution and that this kind of retrospective connection is a construction of contemporary ideology.[29]

Several scholars have pointed out that the modern concept of personal dignity carries traces from an earlier world in which honor and status belonged to a privileged few within secular and ecclesi-astical hierarchies.[30] In a secularizing world, dignity—treating oth-ers respectfully and the feeling that one is entitled to respectful behavior from others—is said to apply equally to all. Justice increas-ingly refers to a sense of belonging (and being recognized as belonging) to the abstract category "human being" regardless of one's condition of life, a status that defines one as having "equal rights before the law"; it refers less to how power and resources are actually distributed in the world—although without careful atten-tion to that matter, the liberal principles of representation, limited government, and citizen rights are easily eroded. "Insult" (part of the genealogy of the law of hate speech as well as of sexual harass-ment) is considered a legal wrong more often than is a substantive inequality—a fact, I suggest, closely connected with the increasing emphasis given to "identity" (a self-owning individual) rather than to unequal structures of power enabled by the modern state.

The concept of dignity has an interesting history in the ways it has been translated from and into different social contexts; what once indicated a high social status is now claimed to be the essence of *all* human beings and thus essential to secular society. But that semantic extension is more complicated than might first be thought. Thus, James Whitman has traced some of the roots of the European Union legalization of that concept to prewar Germany. His startling thesis is that the legal concept of "human dignity" in Europe grew partly out of the fascist-era legal order. He recounts how the fascist regime extended the notion of dignity (*Würde, Ehre*)—ideologically and practically through a system of "honor courts"—to ordinary Germans who had an acceptable claim to membership in society. "Law," writes Whitman, "revolved around the value of 'honour.' "[31]

The equal dignity of all Germans has eventually become the equal dignity of all Europeans. Today dignitary protections for those whom fascists excluded for racial or religious reasons have been driven by revulsion against Nazi practices, but that's not the whole story: "The Nazis extended a claim to honour to the lowest status 'Aryans': they pushed honour down toward the bottom of the social hierarchy. Contemporary jurisprudence has simply continued to push the claim to honour down, reaching at last what were formerly the most despised sectors of the population."[32] Whitman's account reminds us not only that modern dignitary law is compatible with both liberalism and fascism but also that dictatorial regimes can create the conditions for the success of secular claims to equality. As Neal Ascherson recently observed, "Hitler was a moderniser as well as a genocidal tyrant. His perceived legacy is a burden of unbearable horror and humiliation. It's a difficult thought that the Third Reich also contributed to postwar Germany's success in unacknowledged ways: a robust sense of social equality, a stronger sense of common German identity co-existing with the restored federal structure, an imaginative provision for working-class welfare and leisure."[33] This sense of equal dignity, which acquires its density from its place within the modern nation-state, thus has some of its roots—and emotional coloring—in nineteenth-century ideas of race. It not only reinforces the legitimacy and

authority of the nation-state in a world of nation-states, it also helps
to show how easily that notion fits into a state of systematic cruelty.

In the process of modernization and secularization, however,
despotism is not simply a possible enabler of liberal values; liberalism may itself move progressively toward authoritarianism, given
the inability (or unwillingness) of liberals to deal effectively with
economic inequality, its leniency toward political corruption, its
inherent desire to missionize a particular form of life throughout
the world, and its commitment to national security in an ever-
expanding sense—and thus to the necessity of identifying enemies.
"It was Italian fascism," Umberto Eco reminds his readers, "that
convinced many European liberal leaders that the new regime [of
Benito Mussolini] was carrying out interesting social reform, and
that it was providing a mildly revolutionary alternative to the Communist threat."[34] In what used to be called the Third World, there
has long been a political belief that secularism and liberalism may
require despotism and violence. Thus, Hilmi Namnam, a prominent Egyptian journalist and supporter of the July 2013 military
coup in that country, insists: "There is no democracy, no society,
that has progressed without the shedding of blood."[35] Later, in his
capacity as Abdel Fattah al-Sisi's minister of culture, he reaffirms
Egypt's "essentially secular character"—to the anger of Salafis who
were originally allies of those who legitimized Sisi's takeover.

Namnam's notion of "progress" has a recognizable, modern
world–historical sense, quite different from progress as teleology
(i.e., a movement toward a predetermined goal). As Hannah Arendt
explains,

> The notion that there is such a thing as progress of mankind
> as a whole was unknown prior to the seventeenth cen-
> tury, developed into a rather common opinion among the
> eighteenth-century *hommes de lettres*, and became an almost
> universally accepted dogma in the nineteenth. But the

difference between the earlier notions and their final stage is decisive. The seventeenth century, in this respect best represented by Pascale and Fontenelle, thought of progress in terms of an accumulation of knowledge through the centuries, whereas for the eighteenth the word implied an "education of mankind" (Lessing's *Erziehung des Menschengeschlechts*) whose end would coincide with man's coming of age. Progress was not unlimited, and Marx's classless society seen as the realm of freedom that could be the end of history—often interpreted as secularization—of Christian eschatology or Jewish messianism—actually still bears the hallmark of the Age of Enlightenment. Beginning with the nineteenth century, however, all such limitations disappeared.[36]

The use of violence in the imposition of "egalitarianism" (which liberals may regret but claim to find sometimes necessary) and the slide toward authoritarianism (which alarms some liberals but is justified by others on liberal grounds) both share a commitment to a secular national community in which equality must be created or secured.

The ambivalence of egalitarian sentiments might be brought out more clearly if its advocates recognize that in practice the equality aimed at is itself defined by acts of exclusion at once legal and emotional. In a well-known passage, Carl Schmitt, the legal philosopher most liberals excoriate, writes:

> Every actual democracy rests on the principle that not only are equals equal but unequals will not be treated equally. . . . In the democracy of English sects during the seventeenth century equality was based on a consensus of religious convictions. Since the nineteenth century it has existed above all in membership in a particular nation, in national homogeneity. Equality is only interesting and valuable politically so long as

it has substance, and for that reason at least the possibility and risk of inequality.[37]

In the age of European empires, it was politically possible for a relatively homogeneous liberal democracy such as Britain to rule over a heterogeneous population overseas. This fundamental inequality allowed "secularization" to be constructed in different ways in the metropole and in the colonies. Thus, in Britain, the drive for equality derived much of its force from the inequalities of industry and empire that had differential political consequences: in the metropole the concentration of workers in the growing factories, ports, and mines gave them the ability to organize and strike, a political power that helped create more responsive owners of industry and effective calls for social justice. The largely rural colonies, on the other hand, supplied agricultural raw materials for metropolitan factories and served as captive markets, until their populations were mobilized by their upper classes to struggle for independence—that is, for a formal equality with their erstwhile rulers as members of new sovereign states.[38] For all the new possibilities of exercising justice that states acquire at independence, they also acquire the freedom and power to articulate their own exclusions and repressions.

In Europe, whose inhabitants increasingly define their heritage as "Judeo-Christian," the principle of equality within the political community cannot be extended easily to Muslim inhabitants born there because they are identified as the followers of an "illiberal religion"; thus, the claim that secularism requires an absolute neutrality toward its citizens regardless of their faith turns out to be highly problematic. Given God's absence from the world, the secular inheritors of Christianity must appeal not to his equal love for all human beings but to the vital interest of the nation-state: equality is conditional, and dignity limited by international boundaries.

In liberal secular states, equality and dignity seem to be closely tied to the identity of citizen: If one is not the legal member of a territorial state, there are, as Arendt famously argued, no meaningful rights, including the right to dignity. Dignity and equality for "Aryans" meant worthlessness for Jews and Roma. In the secular liberal polity that emerged in eighteenth-century North America as the United States, the self-governing community of equals developed its ideological formation and acquired its material resources by insisting on inequality: African Americans could be included within the community but as unfree labor excluded from civil society, and Native Americans could be massacred and expelled beyond an advancing civilization and thus literally excluded from national territory.[39] But both instances of exclusion were not simply examples of racial separation; they were, more significantly, different strategies of managing and exploiting inferior populations—the one through slavery and the other through reservations.[40] As an emotional disposition and legal status, the equality of citizens therefore has special value when it is contrasted with those subordinated to that privileged circle.

The modern secular world is a system of territorial states with clear borders; there is no space of protection or equality or the enjoyment of dignity for human beings *between* states. The only space where states have no authority, no legal power, is the open sea, a space where human beings are equal in their vulnerability to the elements and therefore in death by drowning. If Christianity has gifted valued secular sentiments to the modern world, the gift is certainly more dangerous than the claim would have us assume because what is most evident in a liberal democratic society is not divine love for all but state power over all.

Sigmund Freud, for whom the experience of social inequality in the modern secular world was replicated in the structure of the mind, saw an endless war involving unconscious "personae" and mental forces, some stronger than others. So it may be said that he provided not only a secular theory of the complex, ambivalent motivations of modern individuals but also a secular model of the forms of deceptiveness and instability characteristic of liberal democracy. The difference, perhaps, is that the process of overcoming self-deception in psychoanalysis has no parallel in politics: the fact that the liberal elite does not know (or want to know) that what it is really saying or doing often leads to disorder and injustice whereas, for the analysand, the completion of analysis eventuates in a condition of greater freedom. That is when the invocation of equality in politics is not merely a challenge but also a ruse.

VI

But perhaps more perplexing about equality is this: Its pursuit (regardless of whether the motivation is religious or secular) can, paradoxically, produce inequality—and, hence, a sense of injustice. Here is a situated story, part history, part fiction.

The United Kingdom has long considered itself to be a secular society although it still has a national church (the Church of England) whose head is the monarch and whose dignitaries are ex-officio members of parliament (House of Lords). This tradition has continued despite the fact that gradually in the twentieth century most legal discriminations practiced against religious minorities have been removed. In that sense Britain's secularization has aimed at greater equality to be attained not by the imposition of Christian unity (centuries of struggle against the Church of England's religious hegemony had long ceased to make that plausible) but by the use of secular reason: what mattered was not one's religious conviction but whether the place one occupied in society matched one's abilities.

In 1958 a novel in the tradition of Aldous Huxley's *Brave New World* was published in Britain, amid much public comment. It dealt with the pursuit of certain kinds of equality defined not only by market competition but also by secular state authority. Michael Young's *The Rise of the Meritocracy* depicts the drive for equality in British liberal democracy since the mid-nineteenth century that encouraged the secularization of social feelings and strengthened the secular language of national politics in opposition to the legal discriminations of state Anglicanism.[41] The novel's narrator offers an explanation of the major crisis of his time—situated in the early 2030s. The crisis is expressed in a violent revolt caused by widespread resentment at the emergence of a society driven by the goal of equality. It was not that everyone had been leveled: society can't do without such asymmetries as teacher and pupil, judge and defendant, doctor and patient, traffic policeman and public traffic as well as the many more who must exercise particular types of authority in particular social situations. The aim was to abolish inequality based on the arbitrary access to authority—that is, access based on familial or religious criteria. Equality of opportunity required that the right to exercise privilege be open to all and established by scientific testing. The result of this revolutionary pursuit of equality, so Young's fictional account goes, is, paradoxically, the emergence of an elite that monopolizes privilege and power in society based on intelligence and capability. Because there is no age of retirement, clear evidence of ability must be sought, and that means continual examinations to test the merit of all who hold given positions lead eventually to the undermining of the very category of seniority. This concept (and, by extension, the authority of experience and tradition) becomes suspect so that, as people's abilities decline with age, the period for which tests (designed by psychologists) are deemed valid becomes progressively shorter. To the extent that the equality of opportunity is systematically applied, the most able rise to the top of society while the least intelligent are left at the bottom. Failures are despised because they are without merit in a society of opportunity, and consequently resentment grows among the majority who find their dignity impugned in the new order. Hence a widespread revolt.

In 1975 Margaret Thatcher spoke of the equality of opportunity as a liberal right in her first speech as leader of the Conservative Party, in Blackpool, U.K.:

> Some Socialists seem to believe that people should be numbers in a State computer. We believe they should be individuals. We are all unequal. No one, thank heavens, is quite like anyone else, however much the Socialists may pretend otherwise. *We believe that everyone has the right to be unequal.* But to us, every human being is equally important. Engineers, miners, manual workers, shop assistants, farm workers, postmen, housewives—these are the essential foundations of our society, and without them there would be no nation. But there are others with special gifts who should also have their chance, because if the adventurers who strike out in new directions in science, technology, medicine, commerce, and industry are hobbled, there can be no advance. The spirit of envy can destroy; it can never build. Everyone must be allowed to develop the abilities he knows he has within him, and she knows she has within her, in the way he chooses.[42]

If, according to this view, everyone has the right to be unequal, it is in one of two very different—but not incompatible—senses: that each person's identity is essentially irreducible to another's and that it is right that everyone should want to try to get ahead of others. Both are *moral* arguments for supporting the principle of equality of opportunity. It is not clear, however, what Thatcher meant by the sentence "every human being is *equally important* to us," whether listeners were to understand this as an expression of sentiment toward everyone or of everyone's value to the functioning of society—although her enumeration of social roles comes almost entirely from the working class and together with her reference to *"others* with special gifts who should also have their chance" clearly reveals her support for class privilege.[43]

Four decades after Thatcher's translation of equality of opportunity into the equal value of different kinds of human beings, Hillary Clinton expressed her commitment to that principle by juggling notions of collective and individual identity: "I know what we are capable of doing together. Together we can break down every barrier holding Americans back, and build *ladders of opportunity for everyone.* America was built by people who had each other's backs, who understood we all have to do our part and that at our best we all rise together."[44] Equal opportunity for everyone to compete, so Clinton believes, allows everyone to rise together—but in hierarchical order. As liberals, both Thatcher and Clinton see the equality of opportunity as a moral right that can and should be translated into a legal right. So here, as reflected in the working of secular reason, the drive for equality of opportunity (i.e., the right to compete) legitimizes inequality as difference. Characteristic of that principle of equality is not merely the belief that the market ensures everyone gets what he or she deserves; the secular drive for equality is presented essentially as the need to promote "difference" as well as efficiency. It is these two non-egalitarian principles that seem to give this call for equality—that is, for meritocracy—its rhetorical force, as opposed to the principle of unconditional mutual care.

In Britain as a whole, so Young's story points out, Christian metaphysics prevails even though the formal practice of Christianity has largely died out. So the discontented ask: "How could men be equal in the eyes of God and yet unequal in the eyes of the Psychologist?"[45] The secular answer to that had to be: While God loves all human beings equally, and at the same time sees each human being as unique, scientific, political, and economic successes demonstrate that all human beings are not equally equipped to occupy any given status. And yet, while the Christian tradition teaches universal compassion and liberal secularity claims to inherit that virtue, political commitment to the equality of opportunity reveals a remarkable failure because it encourages an indifference to forms of cruelty that cannot be adequately addressed by liberal ethics. According to the latter, cruelty is essentially the intentional and gratuitous infliction of pain by someone on another. It doesn't include the cruelty inflicted by a particular form of life on vulnerable humans and other animals—that is, not articulated by an individual intention to kill or make living beings suffer.[46] For different forms of life have their own distinctive ways of letting live and letting die. This includes, for example, what is called in modern warfare "collateral damage" but not "unnecessary cruelty" or "disproportionate violence."

When it is not thought of as the result of what one individual does to another, liberals tend to think of political violence as the principal source of cruelty. But cruelty occurs not only in events such as terrorism and war; it also underlies much of everyday life in the progressive, liberal world. I have mentioned one example of everyday cruelty; here is another: The large urban populations in liberal democracies now have access to plentiful supplies of cheap, nourishing food, thanks to industrial agriculture that has learned how to mass produce animals for meat, milk, and eggs and thus to aim at "welfare for all" although the development regarded as necessary to making food available equally to all citizens involves unprecedented cruelty toward nonhuman forms of life.[47]

In many modern secular states, public demands have been made and laws passed forbidding religious sacrifice of animals on grounds of cruelty.[48] However, the definition of sacrifice as the *unnecessary* killing and hurting of living beings allows the *necessity* of treating animals cruelly—in this case, for the purpose of enhancing social equality. The common liberal condemnation of some acts as "senseless cruelty" implies that there are forms of cruelty that are not senseless. This includes death and serious body injury to citizen soldiers in war formally described as "heroic" when it is seen as a "sacrifice for the nation" and not as a mere "blood ritual."[49] But despite the general prohibition of *all* forms of unnecessary killing, there is an obvious difference in the attitude to the victims in the two cases. In the latter, the victims are ennobled because they and their families suffer death and pain for the sake of the nation; in the former, the victims are produced and consumed as "a lower form of life" in order to reproduce the nation as "a higher form of life." In brief, liberals seem to find it difficult to deal with the inequality that is spelled by cruelty.

VII

So is there a less invidious way of conceptualizing equality? The short answer, according to Jürgen Habermas, is yes, if equality is framed as the possibility of translating religious discourse into secular discourse in the public sphere.

Habermas has famously argued that equality should be extended to religious citizens through the translation of religious discourse in a way that makes equality more inclusive in liberal politics. Instead of confining religious freedom to a private space beyond politics, he proposes that religious discourse be included in the public domain to inspire and strengthen moral commitments in politics. When believers legitimately use their religious language in the public sphere that is dominated by secular language, they are exercising the liberal principle of equality so long as what they say is translatable into a universally understandable language, one therefore accessible to nonbelievers too.[50] Habermas's proposal for translation from religious language (particular and obscure) to a secular one (universal and clear) is intended to strengthen liberal politics by a new argument for a religiosecular pluralism that in fact harks back to the Protestant dissenters of early modernity but is now (hopefully) cleansed of their religious passion and dogmatism by an open-minded attitude supposedly characteristic of cosmopolitanism as a variety of universalism. Habermas and those who follow him have called this theoretical proposal "postsecularism," but arguably it is still part of the attempt to find secular ways of expanding the domain of the political.

Thus, although Habermas wants to see tolerance reflected in the secular state's recognition that citizens have the right to speak as believers in a secular language, he limits the exercise of this right to the informal public sphere where public opinions are expressed, as against parliament where policy decisions are made. Even with this restriction, Habermas stipulates that reasons offered based on religious belief must be accessible to everyone, especially to citizens for whom religious discourse is obscure.

The philosopher Maeve Cooke agrees with Habermas that "any democratic form of political authority must seek to uphold the liberal democratic commitment to freedom and equality," but she doesn't think translation from religious to secular language is the answer. What she thinks *is* essential for that commitment is what she calls nonauthoritarian modes of thinking and acting. A secular society is still, in that sense, a valid aim for Cooke. What seems to me to be at work here is an absolute liberal commitment to emancipation as the essential precondition for valid communication. Given the necessity of the nation-state, Cooke insists that "all political orders are based on certain exclusions and restrictions: the challenge for citizens of liberal democracies is not the elimination of *all* exclusions and restrictions but only those that do not stand up to critical interrogation in public processes of deliberation."[51] This seems at first sight reasonable, but Cooke's view of critical interrogation seems to be entirely discursive, and if I am right in thinking so, the opportunity to engage in it effectively will be denied citizens who lack the leisure and connections to learn the conventions of critical interrogation in public. It also excludes something else of great importance: the body in action. The body not only has its own language; it is also necessary to creating conditions in which others must act. This applies not only to behavior in the domain of war but also to nonviolent protest against state injustice, such as using the citizen's body to anticipate and resist authoritarianism. This will be ruled out on Cooke's criteria even if citizens are educated and articulate and thus able to engage in processes of critical interrogation. And it will not only be ruled out but also very easily, "legitimately" repressed by the state, which finds it easy—relatively speaking—to describe it as "incitement to violence." (In fact, the modern state's monopoly of legitimate violence problematizes the effectiveness of extralegal opposition, whether violent or nonviolent. Radical criticism of the political order, whether it takes a violent or nonviolent form, is effective only when that order is too weak to defend itself.)

Indeed, as everyone involved in practical politics knows, the insistence on "rational dialogue" and "equal respect" is an important tactic of political power. Since time is of the essence for particular problems, the insistence on reasonable dialogue is a way of bypassing particular solutions. Thus, Charles Larmore writes:

> In discussing how to solve some problem (for example, what principles of political association they should adopt), people should respond to points of disagreement by retreating to neutral ground, to the beliefs they still share, in order either to (a) resolve the disagreement and vindicate one of the disputed positions by means of arguments which proceed from this common ground or (b) bypass the disagreement and seek a solution of the problem on the basis simply of this common

> ground. . . . If the people still wish to solve the given problem,
> and if they are committed to solving it through rational dis-
> cussion, then they have no choice but to find the solution on
> the basis of the beliefs they share.[52]

The resemblance of this argument to that of Habermas on postsecularism should be evident, as well as that of John Rawls's idea
of "political liberalism";[53] at any rate, the assumption underlying it
is that "the given problem" is always easy to identify and formulate,
that autonomous individuals on both sides will see the problem and
its solution in the same way.

Actually, for Habermas, "religion" is not simply *translated* in the
course of secularization. "Religion" is first defined (emotionally as
well as intellectually) so that it can be recognized as religion. And
then it is split into two: on the one hand, there is the language and
practice inherited from Christianity that define the secular state
(religion 1), and on the other hand, there is the language and practice of liberal believers who live in a secular society and have rede-
fined their religiosity (religion 2) so that it is entirely compatible
with if not entirely equivalent to the secular. It is in complicated
ways that the former (religion 1) changes the latter (religion 2). Liberal religion is no longer the same as preliberal religion because it
has conceded some of the premises of the secular state and secular
reason in developing new sensibilities and attitudes. So, in Habermas's account, translation is not only said to be a way of making religious and nonreligious citizens equal; it is also the means by which
the secular can lay claim to be the *true* heir to the proper function
of religion in the modern state. There is no place in Habermas's
political world for preliberal religion.

Yet something, Habermas says, is not only gained in the process
of secularization but also lost. The loss is felt as such by nonbeliev-
ing citizens although it cannot be restored in its original form.
Habermas believes that what secularism has achieved must be

preserved, but there is a need for the moral resources that can be made available for a secular state only by what survives as religion— that is, religion 2. Whether the modern state—whose overriding commitment is to maintain itself and its power—is capable of responding to moral suasion, and, if so, then in what language, is a question Habermas doesn't address.

Habermas thinks that what he calls the "inspiring power" of religion is at once necessary for a secular political system and accessible to nonbelievers only in a universal—i.e., secular— language: "Those moral feelings which only religious language has as yet been able to give a sufficiently differentiated expression may find universal resonance once a salvaging formulation turns up for something almost forgotten, but implicitly missed. *The mode for non-destructive secularization is translation.* This is what the Western world, as the worldwide secularizing force, may learn from its own history."[54]

But an unanswered question remains: Does religious "inspiration" come from its divine intent or from the human use of religious stories for new (secular) purposes? Put more directly: Does religious "inspiration" do the same work for nonbelievers as it does for believers? Habermas's response might be: only in the domain of politics. But believers might not want to give politics absolute priority in their life, and they may be reluctant to concede that religious discourse is essentially a means of securing political interest. Must that concern be dismissed?

In the middle of the twentieth century, T. S. Eliot attempted a formulation that embraced both religious and secular senses of the notion of inspiration: "if the word 'inspiration' is to have any meaning, it must mean just this, that the speaker or writer is uttering something which he does not wholly understand—or which he may even misinterpret when the inspiration has departed from him. This is certainly true of poetic inspiration. . . . A poet . . . need not know what his poetry will come to mean to others, and a prophet need not understand the meaning of his prophetic utterance."[55] Eliot's remarks, interestingly, seek to move us away from the question of what decisive *origin* the inspiration reflects (whether "outside" or "inside" the subject) and toward the question of how it *strikes* the subject. He directs us to what the prophet (a "religious" figure) and the poet (a "secular" figure) share: a sense of confronting something that is true and yet something whose full significance may not be understood. Inspiration cannot be translated easily (if at all) precisely because and to the extent that its language is polysemic, indeterminate, and opaque. What exactly the language is doing with the subject—unlocking or locking up particular ways of thinking and acting, responding helpfully to one's helplessness or merely deepening it, say—is not under the control of user or hearer. Habermas's view of translation seems to be the replacement of one word by another (or by a circumlocution) as though it was necessarily an "abstract" cognitive process. The demand for engagement with the sensibilities expressed in poetic or prophetic utterances is ruled out.

There is something else that rebels and prophets and poets—and some novelists and dramatists—share: an invocation of the past not in order to appeal to an impossible return but in order to provoke and challenge the present. Thus, in an interview in 1987, the acclaimed English television dramatist Dennis Potter is asked about the part played by nostalgia in his work. He replies:

> I've used the immediate past to intrude upon the present, so that it isn't a thing out there, the past, which is done with, it is actually running along beside us now, and its, its misconceptions and its values, and its correct conceptions, can be seen just that degree more clearly, and using the forties and the war and the immediate post-war, or in *Pennies from Heaven* the mid-thirties was a way of, without being didactic or preachy or trying to draw political, social, you know, that sort of writing,

just simply letting that time be in order to show what this time is like. So that's the opposite of nostalgia. Nostalgia says it's safety back there, and, Oh those dear dead days and all that, and wrings a tear from your eye, because they are unreclaimable, but I say they are reclaimable and that they are, that they are there and here.[56]

Potter's conception of time is certainly not the familiar linear one in which the past is over and done with, simply the object of disinterested knowledge or sentimental memory. The past, he suggests, is copresent with *now*, for in presenting it on television now, he draws on and reproduces a contemporary sensibility—his own and that of many in his audience. The past is a legitimate object of critique from the standpoint of the present just as the present is an object of critique from the standpoint of the past. At work in Potter's television dramas is a rejection of the idea that time can be neatly packaged into "traditional" (the past) or "progressive" (the future) separated by a shifting line of the present.

Indeterminateness, opaqueness, an evocation of the past, and the impossibility of understanding some discourses without far-reaching shifts in the way one lives and feels and thinks (as even the secular discipline of psychoanalysis recognizes) is not the only feature of language that Habermas ignores. For example, the inequality he identifies is not simply between secular and religious languages. There is difference in his approach to religious languages, only one of which (the language of so-called Judeo-Christianity) is believed to have developed the quality of abstraction necessary for modern knowledge, universal morality, and a truly cosmopolitan order. In contrast, Islam (conceived of as a single historical subject) cannot be a source of inspiration for the modern world because Habermas sees it as the quintessential example of a religious tradition that hasn't been able to adjust to modernity, exemplified, he says, in the terrorist attack of 9/11. What he means by modernity is, of course, a secular world dominated by tamed capitalism (whose primary facilitator of equality, as Marx pointed out long ago in *Capital*, remains *money*), and modern science and technology, and of course the liberal state.[57]

Habermas notes that Buddhism is the only religious language other than the language of Judeo-Christianity that has achieved the level of abstraction necessary for the modern world, but its fatal flaw is that this abstraction is too extreme—it lacks *any* worldly referent. In the West, by contrast, all the valuable aspects of modern life are "the direct legacy of the Judaic ethic of justice and the Christian ethic of love."[58] Habermas's synthesis of two distinct religious traditions reduces a complicated theological history of ethics and the law to two mutually compatible "values," justice and love. Judaism is not seen as a tradition in its own right—including the right to define itself—but as a historical phase of truth that has been superseded by a higher truth (Christianity) and that, in turn, by an even higher one (secularism). Habermas seeing Judaism as an obsolete prelude to Christianity means he doesn't need to address the longstanding Western appeal to St Paul's affirmation of Christian "freedom" and rejection of Jewish "law."[59] He does not need to consider the implications of the Pauline separation between spirit and flesh that, arguably, is not central to Judaism (or for that matter to Islam).

Underlying the Habermasian concept of secularization there seems to be an idea of language as a neutral system for description and argument, not as an aspect of how we inhabit the world. But it is not only what we do with language but also what language does *with* and *to* us that calls for attention.[60] Seen thus, the claim that secular political language can be neutral may just be an attempt to neutralize challenges; the claim that it is the unique carrier of reason, little more than rationalization. If language is part of how we inhabit the world, then an alien language isn't simply a possible source of inspiration for our politics. One might therefore say that an unfamiliar language that actualizes particular ways of living is our equal when we recognize that its obscurity—its resistance to verbal translation—is not necessarily a sign of its poverty or irrationality, or for that matter of not deserving of belief, but an occasion for the listener/reader to think about the limits of our language in imagining and living another form of life. Walter Benjamin once observed in a passage that has since become famous:

> Our translations, even the best ones, proceed from a wrong premise. They want to turn Hindi, Greek, English into German instead of turning German into Hindi, Greek, English. Our translators have a far greater reverence for the usage of their own language than for the spirit of the foreign works. The basic error of the translator is that he preserves the state in which his own language happens to be instead of allowing his language to be powerfully affected by the foreign tongue. . . . He must expand and deepen his language by means of the foreign language.[61]

Translating language is more than a matter of finding verbal equivalents in the language we know best.

VIII

The Habermasian idea of translation of religious language into secular is a way of bringing the religiously committed citizens fully into the public sphere as equal, self-governing agents. For liberals, the question of agency is held to be prior to that of equality. But what Habermas doesn't discuss is that the public/private spaces of agency, a concept central to secularism (and its conception of the proper place of religion) is a modern construction—and one that works invidiously against women.

Joan Scott reminds us of the historical fact that the public:private pair in its various replications (male:female::politics:religion::universal:particular), while being involved in gender inequality, was not, strictly speaking, the imposition of religious power over women. "Rather," she writes, "feminine religiosity was seen as a force that threatened to disrupt or undermine the rational pursuits that constitute politics; like feminine sexuality, it was excessive, transgressive, and dangerous. The danger of feminine sexuality was not taken as a religious phenomenon but as a natural one."[62] It was secularism, Scott points out, that first introduced the idea of gender inequality based on religion.

> Men were individuals, owning that property in the self that enabled them to conclude contracts—including the founding article of political society, the social contract. And men could be abstracted from their physical and social embodiment; that's what the abstract individual was about. Women, in contrast, were dependent, a consequence of the dedication of their bodies to reproduction; they were not self-owning, thus not individuals. And there was no abstracting women from their sex.[63]

Scott emphasizes the fact that secularism has continued to this day to justify gender inequality on "natural" grounds.

Her acute analysis of gender inequality focuses on the so-called problem of headscarves worn by young Muslim women in secular European societies, underlining the contradictions of those who sought to ban it in public, on the grounds that "the veil" was a sign of women's subordination, to ban it in public schools and government spaces. Scott is attentive, as few commentators on this topic have been, to some of the larger psychological problems about equality and agency, and she defends the right of pious young women to wear whatever they want.

In an article published over a decade ago, I noted that perhaps the most interesting aspect of the "*affaire du foulard islamique*" in France was that both those who defended the right to wear the headscarf and those who supported the new law banning it in public spaces (as recommended by the Stasi Commission[64]) approached it as a sign—of a desire to affirm an identity in the former case, and a will suppressed by religion in the latter.[65] As a sign, the headscarf's meaning could be found in the fact that it embodied a motive: "the will to make appear" (*volonté d'apparaître*).[66] Because it was a sign, the headscarf's "real meaning" had to be deciphered, interpreted, and translated into verbal language—as a symbol of inequality. It was *not* to be understood primarily as something the Muslim woman inhabited, part of an orientation, of her way of living.

The commission's concern with the desires of pupils was expressed in a distinction between desires: those who didn't really want to wear the headscarf and those who did. It is not very clear exactly how these "genuine desires" (indicating the will of a self-governing agent) were deciphered, although reference was made to pressure by traditional parents and communities, and one assumes that some statements to that effect must have been made to the commission.[67] However, solicitude for the "real" desires of the pupils applied only to girls who wore the headscarf. No thought appears to have been given to determining the "real" desires of girls who did *not* wear it. It is conceivable that some of them secretly wanted to wear a headscarf but were inhibited from doing so because of what their non-Muslim French peers and people in the street might think or say. Or that unconsciously they simply desired to be "modern." Appearance alone was sufficient for the commission: the absence of a headscarf worn in public means the person concerned has no desire to wear it. "Desire"—the root of agency—is not definitively discovered but semiotically constructed.

Scott draws on the work of feminist scholars, in particular the splendid studies by Phyllis Mack on women's involvement in

Methodism in eighteenth-century Britain and by Saba Mahmood on women and the piety movement in contemporary Cairo, to show that a woman was not necessarily deprived of agency when she tried to live a religious life.

The problem of equality has been connected to the problem of agency because an active self, exercising her *own* will, is seen as a precondition of full equality.[68] My attempt several decades ago to trace aspects of medieval Christian monasticism was directed by this latter problem: A remarkable feature of monastic discipline (and I will turn in the next chapter to an Islamic vision of disciplining virtue) is that it explicitly aims to create, through a program of communal living, the will to obey. The Christian monk who learns to will obedience is not merely someone who submits to another's will because of fear—the traditional norm, at any rate, seeks to refashion an appropriate will/desire. He is not conceived of as someone who has "lost his own will" to the extent that he is a person for whom obedience is *his* virtue—in the sense of his ability to desire a Christian life, a desire that requires the idea of an autonomous agent be set aside.

There is clearly no scientific reason for justifying gender inequality (differential rates of pay, promotion, and access to senior position), but as the examples cited above show, the Habermasian proposal for translating religious discourse into secular is neither necessary for addressing injustice (secular arguments for suppressing women are well known) nor adequate for understanding the problem of agency—that is, an authentic, essentially free-willed self that can exercise its right to be treated as the equal of all within the nation. It also tends to reinforce the distinction between the essential self and its appearance in politics.

2

Translation and the Sensible Body

I

In a book entitled *Translating the Message*, the Christian theologian Lamin Sanneh writes: "It seems obvious that missionary interest . . . in the vernaculars of societies beyond the West touched on the affected cultures in a very profound way. In most of these cultures, language is the intimate, articulate expression of culture, and so close are the two that language can be said to be commensurate with culture, which it suffuses and embodies."[1] Sanneh goes on to say that in using indigenous criteria for translating the Christian message into a non-Christian culture, missionaries have rightly abandoned the original medium in favor of another so that the essential message can be understood and chosen freely. Because the message is detachable, it can be conveyed in and by any medium, and this allows the indigenous languages and cultures in which it is received to flourish. This position, according to Sanneh, contrasts with what he considers to be distinctive of Islam: "Whereas for Christians, mission has come preeminently to mean translation, for Muslims mission has stood consistently for the nontranslatability of its Scriptures in the ritual obligation."[2] Sanneh believes that the form and meaning of prayer can remain the same despite its being translated into a different language. On the other hand, because the language of Islamic prayer is untranslatable from Arabic, the vernaculars that Islam encounters come to be demoted, making the cultural pluralism characteristic of Christianity (and the values that Christianity has bequeathed to modernity) difficult if not impossible for Muslims.

Although Sanneh speaks of nontranslatability in ritual, the thrust of his argument is much wider. One should note, therefore, that it is not the Arabic language as such that is attributed to divinity for Muslims, but Qur'anic enunciation—especially in the context of ritual prayer.[3] Where everyday life is conducted in Arabic, there is no sense that the language is special—nor, for that matter, does the mandatory use of Arabic in ritual preclude "cultural pluralism," if by that term we mean that both Muslims and non-Muslims using Arabic as a means of everyday intercourse (or non-Arabic speaking Muslims abiding by Arabic in their liturgy) are able to live different lives. Sanneh's formulation is of course a way of saying that one cannot be authentically an African if one is also a Muslim, but that one can be African *and* Christian because Christian scriptures and liturgies have been translated into African languages and are thus made at home in African cultures. But more relevant for the present enquiry is that Sanneh suggests Christianity, through its attitude to the translation of sacred texts, paves the way to modernity that Islamic traditionalism prevents. So at first sight Sanneh's position seems to be contrary to Habermas's, for whom postsecularism presupposes that the direction of translation be determined by the politically dominant language—that is, from religious into secular—but they both agree that the meaning of the message is contingently related to its medium.

And yet the question remains: What is the meaning of untranslatability? I cited Jakobson's perception earlier to the effect that, in translating poetry, one is necessarily selecting some values of the original as against others, and in response I asked, "What is poetry?" I then offered the suggestion that "poetry" is the inevitability that language is in *some* measure and in *some* aspects untranslatable. Assuming that is so, how does it help us understand the question of Qur'anic untranslatability?

My first thought here is that the Islamic doctrine of untranslatability may act as a warning against rendering the Book (*al-kitāb*) into no more than a codex (sing. *mushaf*, pl. *masāhif*), against secularizing the Qur'an into a system of signs that is entirely and only in and of the world. As a matter of history, the Qur'an can be engaged with, commented on, and explained in Arabic as well as in non-Arabic languages; there is a rich tradition of Qur'anic interpretation in Islam. Islamic discourse *does* take place through the medium of vernaculars—including demotic Arabic—although then it is, of course, no longer the Qur'an. I recall a weekly radio program when I was in the Sudan in the 1960s, in which Abdullah al-Tayyib, professor of Arabic at the University of Khartoum, explained and expounded Qur'anic verses in Sudanese dialect. For most of the faithful, the Qur'an must be recited only in the original Arabic in ritual performances. Abdallah al-Tayyib's radio talks didn't suggest otherwise, and I never heard of ritual recitations being performed in Sudan in other than the original—although the Kemalist attempt at encouraging prayers in modern Turkish for secular reasons is well documented.[4]

In the discussion following a presentation by Jacques Derrida at a conference in Paris on religion and media in 1998, I spoke of the question of Qur'anic untranslatability as "fundamental," to which Derrida responded in a way that seemed to me an interesting misunderstanding of my point:

> What you say is fundamental. It is essentially tied to all the fundamentalisms, in particular, in the Islamic areas. Nowhere else is the attachment to the untranslatable letter, the letter

of the Qur'an, so inflexible. There is to be sure, a certain religion of the idiom, everywhere, even within Christianity: French [Catholic] fundamentalism distinguished itself at a certain moment in time through its defense of Latin in the prayer service. But nowhere, it seems to me, does the *fixed* literalness of language, the idiomatic form of the original message, in its very body, sanctify itself to the extent it does in the Moslem religion.[5]

This seems to suggest that "fixed literalness" is an essence that helps to define "the Moslem religion." What I think Derrida overlooks is a distinction that the Islamic tradition makes for the purpose of scholarly knowledge (*fiqh*) between *nass*, "literal text" (or *muhkam*, "precise, clear text"), and *mutashābíha*, "obscure or metaphorical text," and the situational importance of each that requires interpretation in the understanding of Qur'anic language. This distinction partly overlaps another that is crucial: its exoteric sense (extracted by the interpretive process called *tafsīr*) and its exegetical sense (extracted by the explanatory process called *ta'wīl*).[6]

II

Most Muslim theologians have stressed the doctrine of the inimitability of the Qur'an as a reason for the Muslim reluctance to translating it. And yet the Qur'an has been translated—into about seventy languages since the sixteenth century, although they are not regarded, strictly speaking, as "translations" of the divine word but as interpretations of its meaning.[7] My suggestion—intended neither as a refutation nor as a justification of the Muslim doctrine of Qur'anic inimitability—is that instead of beginning with the question "How can we explain the Qur'an's untranslatability," we should begin descriptively, as believers do, with the reverential attitude on the part of the believer toward the Creator, an act that combines feeling and act, public visibility and private thought.

As a preliminary, one may say that the special attitude toward the Qur'an is an expression of the distinction between the absolute authority of God's word and its human interpretation that is inevitably vulnerable to error. This distinction lies at the base of two problems: (1) How is textual authority thought of in what is known in English as "Islamic jurisprudence" (*fiqh*), and (2) what is Qur'anic utterance in ritual worship supposed to do?

In his valuable essays on Islamic law and ethics, Baber Johansen has pointed out that Joseph Schacht, Christiaan Snouck Hurgronje, and others who are regarded in the West as founders of the modern study of Islamic jurisprudence (*fiqh*), have seriously underestimated the scope and significance of doctrinal disagreements between the schools and how this was connected to human error. Precisely because dissent on details is not regarded as heresy,

the respect for normative pluralism (*ikhtilāf*) is possible only because the *fiqh* scholars conceive an ontological difference between the knowledge as revealed by God in Koranic texts, the prophet's praxis or the community's consensus on the one hand, and the knowledge which human beings acquire through their own reasoning. The first one contains absolute truth, the second one is fallible human reasoning. The second one has to interpret the first but cannot aspire to reach its rank. Therefore the *fuqahā* recognize the contingency of all results of scholarly reasoning. The acknowledgment of the contingency of all human acts and forms of reasoning is at the basis of the *fiqh* as a discipline which compromises [sic] different methods and schools of thought (*madhāhib*) and different organizations of scholars and upholds the cohesion of the scholars and doctrines.[8]

The critical point here, therefore, is not simply the absolute authority of God's word but the unavoidability of human uncertainty—as expressed in the process of translation/interpretation. This view is also reflected in the reluctance by most practicing Muslims to accept an "authoritative" translation of the Qur'an, although translations into languages other than Arabic have been around for centuries, and to insist on the special status of the original as untranslatable in the ritual context.[9]

The nontranslatability of the Qur'an signals that it is to be regarded as a revelation—and revelation, as Eliot pointed out, is like poetic inspiration: difficult if not impossible to translate. It has to be approached on its own terms, and it is not always easy to determine what these are. To the extent that the Qur'an is taken to be the word of God, reverence and gratitude toward it by the believer are presupposed in approaching it, and this is expressed in rules of purity when touching the physical book as well as in the care that the Word remain inviolate in written or verbal transmission. I stress that my argument is not that it is impossible for, say, a Turkish Muslim to experience a sense of awe and reverence when reading a Turkish translation of the Qur'an; my suggestion is that reciting the Qur'an in the original especially in a liturgical context is thought to be a particular (physical-emotional-cognitive) attitude, that its nontranslatability has a special significance intrinsic to *this* sense. It is not the Arabic *language* that is sacred but the enunciation of divine virtues in the presence of what is believed to be a transcendent, creative power. That is to say, it is the act of worship (not the Qur'anic *text*) that is nontranslatable, whose full sense is not given in a dictionary (even a dictionary that provides an explanation of seventh-century Arabic in modern Arabic) but one that requires cultivation. The Arabic used in everyday life—whether by Muslims or by Christians—is not regarded in any sense as "holy."

Another point, to which I shall return, is this: the nontranslatability of the Qur'an in a liturgical context makes it difficult for

political as well as ecclesiastical authority to control Qur'anic meaning. The original is always present, generating unlimited possibilities of meaning.[10] Qur'anic texts translated into national languages
for use in liturgy both grows out of and reinforces the primacy of the
"national community" and the authority of the state that represents
it—a secular motivation if ever there was one. Nontranslatability
sits uneasily with the ambition of state power and the pervasiveness
of capitalist exchange.

III

The claim that understanding discourse always requires that it be
abstracted belongs to a particular language ideology according to
which a message can always be separated from its medium, that the
act of recitation be considered identical to the sheer presence of the
text. The English philosopher R. G. Collingwood suggested nearly
a century ago that it was probably true to say every articulation had
what he called its "own emotional charge." He suggested, nevertheless, that one could learn to "sterilize" one's feelings in particular
cases (to abstract them cognitively)—a habit that, in his view, was
"especially characteristic of adult and 'educated' people in what is
called modern European civilization."[11] Collingwood used the common English word "feeling" precisely because it covers a range of
modalities: from sensing heat or cold, through experiencing anger
or envy, to desiring a person or object, to speaking "unemotionally,"
and so on. All feelings, he argued, were at once experiences and
expressions of experience. This is a useful move to the extent that
it reminds us that "feelings" are not only rooted in the sensible body;
they are also states of "preconsciousness" in which all animals,
including humans, live. But its capacious sense makes it close to the
problematic modern usage of "emotion" and thus may obscure particular states of the body and mind in action, in some of which

feeling is simply a sensation with or without awareness of it; in others, feeling and thought are contingently related so that the former may sometimes obscure or distort the latter, and in yet others feeling is constitutive of action and neither its cause nor its effect. In this latter sense we get the possibility not only of one's feelings being "sterilized" (apparently removed from one's statements and actions) but also of the ability to learn or be taught *particular* feelings that are integral to particular actions. This means that although feeling/emotion can be *theoretically* abstracted from particular utterances, it cannot actually be separated from them. As Robert Solomon has argued in *The Passions: Emotions and the Meaning of Life*, this tendency to separate emotion has also led, since early modernity, to a conceptual opposition between thinking and feeling, although the latter lumps together a great variety of distinctive thoughts and acts.[12] And it is this abstraction that has led to the constitution of a modern category called emotion.[13] An important consequence is the appropriation of the concept of emotion by the modern concept of "aesthetics," and away from "ethics," "faith," and "politics." Nevertheless, what one can learn from Collingwood is that feeling is not absent from what one thinks of as "objective" statements but different from other statements because feeling pervades all language and at the same time articulates the sensing body. The claim that some utterances are "unemotional" or "detached" or "cold" indicates a contextual contrast and not an absolute lack.

Incidentally, T. S. Eliot had claimed in 1921 that the separation of thought from feeling—for which he coined the term "dissociation of sensibility"—first emerged in England in the poetry of the later seventeenth century and thus facilitated the process of secularization. Typical of the best of those later called "metaphysical poets," writes Eliot, was the "direct sensuous apprehension of thought, or a recreation of thought into feeling." For John Donne, for example, a thought was an experience that modified his sensibility. In the seventeenth century, poets increasingly displayed a dissociation of sensibility, the separation of thought and feeling, particularly under the influence of two major intellectual poets: John Milton and John Dryden. This led, says Eliot, to the sentimental age of the eighteenth century, when poets rejected the analytic, descriptive language used by the latter. "Those who object to the 'artificiality' of Milton or Dryden sometimes tell us to 'look into our hearts and write," observes Eliot. "But that is not looking deep enough; Racine or Donne looked into a good deal more than the heart. One must look into the cerebral cortex, the nervous system, and the digestive tracts."[14]

It was the momentous emergence of the scientific revolution in the seventeenth century that helped to crystalize the distinction between feeling and language.[15] In previous centuries "experience" was taken to be the ground from which knowledge of natural regularities could be asserted; by the end of the seventeenth century "experience" itself came to be seen as capable of being disciplined and re-presented through measurement and calculation—a critical step in the development of secular reason.[16] The mathematization of "experience" (henceforth known in English as "experiment") was a way of "sterilizing" feeling, of separating the intellect from what was supposed to be inessential to it for genuine knowledge—that is, of disciplining an objectively oriented, knowing self in a disinterested way. For the new science, what could not be calculated did not, strictly speaking, qualify as knowledge. Paradoxically, together with the growth of disinterested scientific knowledge, nascent capitalism helped produce the self-interested subject. But in early modern Europe, the idea of "disinterestedness" primarily served, together with ideas of science, nature, and objectivity, to reinforce the politics and aesthetics of order. Subsequently, however, skepticism directed at 'natural order" and "scientific objectivity" helped complicate the idea of disinterest, and disinterest (in the form of altruism, charity, etc.) eventually acquired a more positive sense, opposed to self-interest as a natural disposition.

The attitudes toward disinterest and self-interest of both religiously and secularly committed persons shifted and overlapped as
society changed. In early modern England "disinterest" was part of
a network of meanings that included "indifference," "neutrality,"
"equilibrium," and "absence of desire/appetite," thus making it easy
to shift from one sense to another.[17]

IV

Every good translator knows how paradoxical the process of translation can be, but here I want to pursue the thought—contrary to
Sanneh's familiar comments about Qur'anic discourse—that it *is*
translated not simply into other words but into life, that is, into
practices in the context of a particular tradition of ritual and disciplining of the soul. Qur'anic language is believed to be an educative discourse, and therefore an openness is expected on the part
of the subject to be educated into and by an entire discursive
tradition.

I suggested that resistance to translating Qur'anic language
recited in daily, prescribed prayers (or ritual commitments) has to
do with the sense that a verbal translation might begin a process of
deritualization by treating translation as essentially a move from
one set of signs to another. So how should one think about the
translation of Qur'anic language to the sensible human body? For
language is not only what we do with it (as J. L. Austin famously
argued in *How to Do Things with Words*, in 1962) but also what it does
to us and *in us*.

In traditions that deny God can ever take on a material body,
that regard the representation of God to be inconceivable, that
reject the idea of divine incarnation, that make a sharp distinction
between God the Creator and His creation, human divinity is
a grammatical impossibility: God's eternal word, it is believed,

cannot be confused with the life of a finite body.[18] This makes the translation of God's word into the sensible human body problematic. Medieval Muslim theologians famously debated the status of the Qur'an in terms of the distinction between God's essence and His attributes. The form the argument took was over whether the Qur'an was created (i.e., the product of a pure agent) or uncreated (i.e., coeval with God because God's language is part of Him and therefore not part of His creation). Thus, for the rationalist movement known as Mu'tazila, the primary concern was God's absolute unity, which led rationally to the exclusion of "God's attributes" mentioned in the Qur'an because the apparent anthropomorphism seems to undermine that unity. However, according to Hanbalis (followers of one of the four mutually recognizing Sunni schools of law and ethics), a primary purpose of the Qur'an is to recite it in adoration of God whose quasi-human attributes (the Merciful, the Compassionate, the Wise, the Forgiving, the Friend, etc.) are essentially human ideals. In opposition to Mu'tazili rationalism, Hanbalis took the view that reading (qara'a, to read, to recite) the Qur'an is essentially an act of trust (imān, "faith") toward a power infinitely greater than human beings and uniquely perfect. Reciting it is therefore the recognition of ideals (mercy, compassion, wisdom, forgiveness, friendship, etc.) that humans so often fail to achieve. In being recited, the Qur'an was not simply a divine communication but an affirmation of those ideals as originating in God in the presence of God.

The widespread practices in the Muslim world aiming at the literal incorporation of God's word into the body or affixing it to the body in the form of amulets with a view to curing sickness or ensuring safety are legitimized or denounced as echoes of that debate. One widespread practice in Muslim societies consists of drinking verses of the Qur'an that are written on a wooden board and then washed off with water, which is then ingested. In his fascinating study of Qur'anic schools in West Africa, historian and ethnographer Rudolph Ware writes of this practice among young schoolboys as the eternal Qur'an incorporated into finite human beings.[19] This practice (and others like it) is perhaps reminiscent of the Christian sacrament of the Eucharist—which I have heard some Muslims give as a reason for denouncing it.[20] Ware also cites reports (strongly contested by most Sunni scholars) that individuals drank the Prophet's blood when he was cupped, as evidence of the desire by his companions to incorporate God's word literally through the Prophet's body—who has been described by one tradition as "The Walking Qur'an."[21] The emphatic Qur'anic prohibition against drinking blood and against blood on one's person—in the Islamic tradition, a major source of impurity disqualifying one from, among other things, contact with the Qur'an—are opposed within the tradition according to the interpretation given by those whose practice Ware describes. My purpose here is not, of course, to dispute Ware's account of the tradition (to assert what is or is not essential to it) but to point to the existence of a dispute about Qur'anic translation within a tradition, a dispute between sides that draw differently on secular and theological reasons.

In brief, translation in the Islamic tradition does not occur directly from divinity to the believer's body; it occurs from traditional representations of the Prophet's life—that is, accounts of his sayings and actions transmitted down the years by a chain of named individuals beginning with his companions. Together with the words of the revealed Qur'an, these textual accounts are a major Islamic source that has been translated from the Arabic into the local languages of Muslims in various parts of the world—and thence into behavior patterns regulated and taught by Islamic tradition.[22] The ultimate authority of these accounts resides in the Qur'an, which repeatedly commands the faithful to follow the Prophet, and it is the Prophet who sets up the paradigm of prayer in which verses of the Qur'an are recited together with repeated bodily movements expressing submission and reverence toward God.

V

How do such ideas of translation from the Qur'an compare with Christian ideas? A well-known story about the formation of the Christian tradition, repeated by Sanneh, is relevant: By abandoning the idea of Jerusalem as its worldly center, Christianity encouraged the growth of multiple religious centers in different parts of the Hellenized world—and consequently the direct translation of the divine message into different languages. Furthermore, nascent Christianity was able to integrate Greek philosophical categories into its own tradition.[23] To the extent that this story is significant, it indicates that we do not always regard historical time as a neutral medium for conveying a retrievable message and culture but as a process of eventualization that determines—and sometimes distorts—not only ideas but also ways of life. This story stands, so Sanneh tells us, in stark contrast with Islam, which was not Hellenized and enriched as Christianity was.[24]

This account must be qualified, however, in light of a large body of research into the history of ideas. To begin with, in its early phase the Islamic tradition was also an inheritor of Eastern Mediterranean thought and practice, as was early Christianity—albeit in different ways.[25] Thinking about these and other religious traditions as autonomous needs to be reconceived as traditions simultaneously occupying a single, complex, intellectual, and social field in the lands surrounding the Eastern Mediterranean, in which each responded to the others, disagreeing or agreeing and reformulating what became distinctive, yet partly linked (if often mutually antagonistic) traditions.[26] In this historical context, translation is often "prejudiced," in the sense that it seeks out plausible linguistic reasons for identifying some possible meanings at the expense of others not only in order to assimilate or condemn the discourse to be translated but also to legitimize the evolving tradition (or dissenting part of a tradition) for which the translation is destined. Orientalists have long tried to trace Jewish and Christian "origins" of Islam, but virtually nothing has been done on the influence of Islamic tradition on the development of Judaism and Christianity.

The point I wish to stress here is that by absorbing aspects of earlier traditions, Islam, as well as Christianity, acquired not merely theoretical knowledge (as conveyed in philosophical traditions) nor simply an emphasis on the value of contemplation but a practice exemplified in what the Greeks called *paideia*, the education of young aristocrats for roles they would need to perform in their society.[27] This meant learning to cultivate behavior through a process that can be termed ritualization by its correction and repetition.

In medieval Christendom this philosophical tradition was carried by monasticism, a spiritual practice invented in pre-Islamic Egypt. Thus, Jean Leclerc:

> In the monastic middle ages, as well as in antiquity, *philosophia* designated not a theory or a way of knowing, but the experience of wisdom, a way of living according to reason. Now there are two ways to live according to reason. Either one lives it according to the wisdom of this world that the pagan philosophers taught (the *philosophia saecularis* or *mundialis*), or one lives it according to Christian wisdom that is not of this world but already of the future (*philosophia caelestis* or *spiritualis divina*). The philosopher par excellence, and even the philosophy, is Christ, in whom the wisdom of God is incarnate (*ipsa philosophia Christus*).[28]

In the Islamic tradition this idea of living according to reason is exemplified most famously, and influentially, in the major work of the jurist, theologian, and mystic Abū Hāmid al-Ghazālī, *The Revival of The Religious Sciences* (*Iḥyā 'ulūm addīn*).

VI

According to Ghazālī, the soul (*nafs*) is a set of potentialities at birth (*nafas* means "breath") that becomes a self (*nafs*) only gradually and with the help of others. This idea belongs in part to a particular spatiotemporal domain (the Eastern Mediterranean, from about 500 BCE up to about 1000 CE) in which various traditions coexisted. But Ghazālī differs crucially from Aristotle: he does not consider, as the latter does, that *thinking* is the essence of the self and that, therefore, a life of contemplation is its supreme achievement. For Ghazālī, it is the self as created by and learning to orient itself toward God (and, hence, toward his creatures) that is central.

That is why Ghazālī deals in detail with all aspects of human living: from such banal matters as proper manners for eating and drinking to contemplating the completion of life in death. In this tradition, the life of this world doesn't clearly separate "religion" from "nonreligion." It is precisely an achievement of secularism that makes "religion" an autonomous domain and "religious discourse" a technical language. Thus, the solemnity of daily prayer (*ṣalāt*) is articulated by a paradigmatic intention shared with charitable acts (*zakāt*) that is not, in the same sense, solemn. More important, what is prescribed (*wājib*) and what is forbidden (*harām*) do not together comprehend the entirety of "religious" life.

The first reason is that there are other categories in the tradition than positive and negative commands: *makrūh* (disapproved) and *mustahab* (approved). This suggests that the shari'a should not be translated by the word "law" as understood in the modern world because it includes justiciable as well as nonjusticiable matters, injunctions to act according to valid rules of appropriate behavior as well as methods for securing valid rules (epistemology). That doesn't mean, however, that in the shari'a law and ethics are "confused" (as some Orientalists have maintained) because that would imply the two are essentially distinguishable, whereas their constitution as conceptually independent domains is a relatively recent historical development.

The second reason is the existence in the shari'a of a mediating category, *mubāh*. *Mubāh* refers not merely to what is permitted but also to what is free and open to everyone: indifferent forms of existence. Ghazālī uses the term *'amal* (pl. *a'māl*), which is usually translated into English as "action," but since *'amal* includes rest as well as movement, whereas "action" carries the sense of energy expended in doing something—hence "passion" as the state of being acted upon—this common translation seems to me inadequate, and "mode of existence" preferable. Hence his focus on the narrower class of *a'māl* discussed in the section entitled "States of being articulated by intention."[29] What matters to Ghazālī are states embodying or promoting piety or venality—or as neither (as *mubāh*).

Because *mubāh* points to what falls outside the categories of forbidden (*harām*) and mandatory (*wājib*) because its contents cannot be exhaustively enumerated, its limits are indeterminate. *Mubāh* includes but is not exhausted by casual conversation, pleasurable activities, the accumulation of various kinds of information and inventions, the routines and habitual activities of everyday life (*'ādah*). Such activities may generate a desire for coherence within a particular genre or in life conceived of as a whole. But because practices that are *mubāh* also affect and shape desires, they may be pulled into one or other of the evaluative categories, whether positive or negative. It is at this juncture that the nonjusticiable categories of *makrūh* (disapproved) and *mustahab* (approved) come into

play, making "forbidden" (*harēm*) or "mandatory" behavior (*wājib*)—
that is, absolute categories of behavior—eventually graspable. Since
virtues and vices are absolute, Ghazālī insists that one cannot con-
vert the latter into the former by producing a benign intention—as
though intention was a cause of action.[30]

There is no single principle for the exercises that Ghazālī
recommends—other than ultimate orientation to God—and so the
exercises range from acts of worship (*'ibādāt*), such as daily prayers,
annual fasting, charity, and so on, to everyday behavior. In each
case the reasoning deployed is particular to the matter discussed.
The Arabic word "*nafs*" has been translated as both "soul" and
"self," but strictly speaking the sense of "self" as used in common
(and scholarly) discourse in our day is not what Ghazālī means by it,
so I usually read it as "soul": implying a set of divinely implanted
potentialities and tendencies within which there are continuous tensions but always containing the possibility of awareness of what one
is in the fullest sense. The tradition Ghazālī invokes recognizes multiple temporalities: time as the apportionment of particular events,
time as the experience of gradual learning, and time as the death that
culminates and retrospectively defines for others a particular life.

The self can't realize itself on its own: it is formed in time through
a discursive tradition by means of third-person perspectives (i.e.,
of persons other than those with whom one interacts directly). The
self's dependence on others—for everyday projects as well as for
completing its potentialities—is essential, and both learners and
those who have trodden this path successfully earlier can judge
between success and failure. Ghazālī's ethical vocabulary deals with
the dynamics that constrain or facilitate the formation of a virtuous soul. Human beings, Ghazālī says, have an inborn yearning to
achieve a divine form but must dwell as animal bodies in this world.
The yearning, the awareness, and the realization of the virtues are
all made possible only through the body's senses that are intrinsic
to reasoning within and about relations with others.[31]

For Ghazālī, humans are animals distinguished from nonhuman animals by two connected qualities: knowledge (practical and theoretical) together with will or intention (both translations of *irāda*) to be understood as a practical orientation to an object.[32] When a person is aware of the necessity and consequence of a mode of existence, he says, a strong desire (*irāda*) is aroused in him or her to achieve *that* end, thus making desire willful. It is when the sense of "will" shifts from being an *orientation* (toward or away from a transcendental power) to being an *origin* (the agent's causal energy) that one might say a move is made toward secularity. For Ghazālī, willful desire (as opposed to stubbornness) is possible only because, unlike animals, humans possess at birth the capacity for faith (*imān*) as well as reasoning (*'aql*), where faith is a matter of trusting God and reasoning gives one access to the ways particular choices help to shape desires.

Ghazālī's use of the Arabic word " *'aql*" is not the same as the common use of the English word "reason" that is usually given as its translation: *'aql* ranges from the most banal sense experiences (apprehensions) of the finite human being to the most esoteric realization of transcendent truth that the human soul is capable of; desiring what is virtuous depends on both reason and passion (passionate reasoning). Desire, lust, appetite, passion are all possible English translations of the Arabic word "*shahwa*," depending on how the relevant context is identified. They aim at obtaining what the body needs to reproduce itself and to flourish in a particular way of life, and reasoning is essential to it. But one may satisfy and express one's desires, appetites, passion in vicious ways as well as virtuous. Confronting reason in all its instances, the soul contains a force that Ghazālī calls "satanic" (*shaytāniyya*) that prevents the human being from recognizing his "true" desires—that is, not necessarily those the individual *thinks* he has. In every soul there is therefore a continuous struggle between the attempt at realizing virtuous modes of being and the force that opposes them. In other words, there is a continuous conflict between the attempt to establish a successful connection between real understanding and being, on the one hand, and, on the other hand, the force that seeks to distort and undermine the latter.

In the tradition Ghazālī invokes (and contributes to), there is a "soul that urges evil" (*an-nafs al-ammāra bi-ssū'*, Qur'an 12:53) and a "blaming or criticizing soul" (*bi-nnafsi-l-lawwāmati*, Qur'an 75:2), the tendency to mislead oneself, on the one hand, and to block that tendency through increasing awareness as well as correction by relatives and friends, on the other. To reject evil is therefore as important for Ghazālī as following virtue. Exercising the soul requires continually asking oneself what it is one is doing and wanting to do, trying to ensure that one is not deceiving oneself. It is only because of this that continuous repetition in behavior and self-questioning when one encounters evil are essential. In this tradition, self-understanding, with the help of others (beginning with the help of God himself), is central. And yet failure threatens the virtuous formation of the soul at every moment. And while teachers and friends should correct one another for faulty behavior, Ghazālī reprimands those who go to extremes in criticizing others.

In short, Ghazālī's understanding of exercising the soul presupposes both an appropriate desire as well as appropriate techniques for trying to fulfill the desire. Interestingly, for him as for other Sufis, awareness of the truth is typically expressed through the word "taste" (*dhawq*), a sense that includes the pleasure of ingesting food and the reverence in reciting God's word (to both of which the tongue is central) and thus approaching esoteric truth. Learning to "taste the truth" is not an instance of translating verbal signs into nonverbal sign systems but simply learning to "realize the truth" as feeling-and-attitude. Most commentators on Ghazālī, incidentally, take "taste" to be "a metaphor," but since taste is a form of touch, it is part of a complicated history of sense awareness that links it with the truth of certain states of being. I would suggest that attention to this history offers a more interesting reason for the use of the word "taste" than a hasty resort to the idea of metaphor precisely because "taste" encompasses the sense of touching and being touched and of how the enunciation of revelation touches one. Not only divine language but all language has the potentiality of articulating feelings, especially when it seizes and moves the sensible body.

In this tradition it is not merely what one learns to *say* in disembodied words but how one learns *to live* in and through language and silence that expresses the central point of an encompassing vision: humility in one's own successful learning and a showing, not a proving, to others of a form of life that prods them to reexamine their own life and provides them with reasons for changing it in a truthful direction. For Stoics, this meant principally living according to nature; for Christians, it meant the imitation of Christ.[33] The process of learning how to live by reference to a transcendent vision (through practical knowledge[34]) is central, incidentally, not only to the Islamic, Christian, and Judaic traditions but also, in very different ways, to Buddhism, Taoism, and Hinduism.

Michel Foucault and others have famously written about the "care of the self," but in contrast to individualistic formulations of that process, my emphasis here is on how the self gradually learns to develop its abilities from within a tradition that presupposes generational collaboration in the preservation, teaching, and exercise of practical knowledge that is rooted in a vision of the good life. In his later work, Foucault was inspired by the great historian of classical antiquity Pierre Hadot, who in turn admired Foucault's work but also disagreed with him over the idea of care of the self. Thus, Hadot writes:

What I am afraid of is that, by focusing his interpretation too exclusively on the culture of the self, the care of the self, and conversion toward the self—more generally, by defining his ethical model as an aesthetics of existence—M. Foucault is propounding a culture of the self that is *too* aesthetic. In other words, this may be a new form of Dandyism, late twentieth-century style. This, however, deserves more attentive study than I am able to devote to it here. Personally, I believe firmly—albeit perhaps naively—that it is possible for modern man to live, not as a sage (*sophos*)—most of the ancients did not hold this to be possible—but as a practitioner of the ever-fragile *exercise* of wisdom.[35]

Aestheticization in this context claims not only the right to exercise individual judgment but also the individual's right to exercise ultimate authority over herself independently of a discursive tradition. Stefan Collini, a historian of nineteenth-century ideas, has described the Romantic self as a self detached from any tradition: In Romanticism such a self reflects an attitude that "suggests an openness to experience, a cultivation of the subjective response, an elevation of the aesthetic and an exploratory attitude towards one's own individuality and potential, all of which carry a different, perhaps more self-indulgent, certainly more private, message and political bearing."[36] This kind of conception of the self was incidentally the target of St. Augustine's famous warning fifteen centuries earlier: "Hands off yourself; try to build up yourself and you build a ruin." Ghazālī would certainly have endorsed Augustine's position if he had known of it because, for him, there is no essential self that can guide itself; there are only potentialities of the soul that can be realized through or against a living tradition.

And yet in particular niches of modern culture there are echoes—secular versions—of a living tradition that provides models of means and ends. Thus, the professional actor tries to set herself aside and inhabit the somatic and mental world of her character—her gestures, passions, and desires. The actor's agency consists not in the actions of the role she performs but also in her ability to disempower herself for the sake of another. Her ability to act is not solely her own. It is her own *and* that of the dramatist who has written the script, of the director who mediates between script and performance, of other actors, and, not least, of the vibrancy (or its lack) between performance and audience. Her perfected ability belongs, therefore, to the tradition of acting in which she has been schooled and which she tries to develop—perhaps in some measure by reacting against it. Thus, the actor's interpretation and performance of the script depends on a number of coagents past and present, but it is misleading to say that her actions are not entirely her own. The fact that she is not the author of the story doesn't mean she is a passive, subordinated subject who has given up her own agency.

VII

I have been arguing that, unlike certain modern views of language translation, the traditional Muslim position on this question is not necessarily evidence of the devaluation of non-Arabic languages, still less an indifference toward the divine message delivered in the Qur'an, as modernists imply. What that position suggests, I think, is something more interesting: a concern about secularization, a worry that abstracted intellectual meanings of the text will displace its relation to the reading/reciting/religious self. It assumes that certain messages cannot be separated from the medium because *how* the medium comes to inhabit the subject and engage her is crucial to what they mean. In other words, for devout Muslims, Qur'anic meanings are not mechanically determined by logical and lexical criteria or even simply by social context. Piety as awe of God (*birr wa taqwa*) is not merely a divine injunction; it is regarded as a necessary presupposition for arriving at the meanings of the Qur'an. Like the icon for believing Christians, the divine recitation intimates a form of life within but also beyond the present, something that may be lost but can be re-evoked and confirmed as it crystallizes in the heart of the faithful man or woman.[37] That form of life is a development of sensibilities—as indicated by the word "*taqwa*," usually translated as "piety," since *taqwa* also has the sense of "strengthening."

I want now to elaborate on this point by exploring the idea of ritual and ritualization, often regarded as the quintessence of tradition, whether religious or nonreligious. Theories of ritual have been central to the early history of anthropology. In more recent times, most of these theories have been based on a fundamental distinction—made famous by Edmund Leach—between instrumental and symbolic actions, where ritual is seen not as attempting to *do* something to the natural world but as *symbolizing* something.[38] Theories that distinguish between instrumental and symbolic actions still surface from time to time. A sophisticated example is Stanley Tambiah's *A Performative Theory of Ritual*, which draws on J. L. Austin and John Searle to develop an elaborate definition of ritual as "social communication, of . . . a special kind."[39]

In what follows, however, I want to shift the discussion from the social functions of ritual action to its structure and how that might articulate the agent's feelings, thoughts, and attitudes. The idea of ritualization, I suggest, can help us focus on the way the agent attempts to form appropriate feelings and thoughts in particular action and how the action can be seen as a moment in the formation of the self.

I stress that I am not interested in presenting a theory of "ritual." I regard ritual as a "family concept" because its usage variously interconnects and overlaps with that of convention, formula, formalization, repetition, compulsiveness, instinct, coercion, play, and so on. And since all language is variously embedded in social life, family concepts are continuously reconstructed and shifted as forms of life change.

VIII

I turn to Paul Powers's useful study of intent (*niyya*) in medieval Islamic shari'a manuals—and particularly to the first half of his book that deals with intention in the mandatory daily prayers (sing. *salāt*, pl. *salawāt*). I choose Powers partly because he finds the recent publication by anthropologists Caroline Humphrey and James Laidlaw, *The Archetypal Actions of Ritual*, inspiring for his own understanding of Islamic worship.[40]

Humphrey and Laidlaw define ritual as "prescribed acts" and emphasize the importance of the rules that constitute them. They note that, although rituals are not accidental or random acts, they do not depend intrinsically on the intention or feeling of persons performing them and that, as formal acts, they are "discrete, named entities"—each with a beginning and an ending—and therefore real as rituals.[41] This seems to make the rituals "thing-like" in the classic Durkheimian sense, although Humphrey and Laidlaw are quick to distance their position from what they understand to be Émile Durkheim's by noting that in talking about ritual they are concerned with the actions of thinking beings: It is not enough, they write, "to see the actions from outside, as objective 'social facts' in the Durkheimian tradition which Mauss helped to found. But people are also conscious of their actions. While we argued in Chapter 4 that the intention with which a person performs a ritual act does not give their action identity or meaning, we tried to stress that such a person does, none the less, act intentionally."[42] Of course people are conscious of their actions (*always* conscious if that is a logical precondition of "human action"), but, as I pointed out above, "consciousness" in the sense of *thinking* that Aristotle regards as the real part of the self is not the same as the "consciousness" (in the sense of being awake, alert) that Ghazālī identifies as crucial—nor is "consciousness" the indeterminate mental state that modern genetic psychology (starting with the nineteenth-century philosopher Franz Brentano[43]) replaced by the internally structured concept of "intention" as a mental event directed at an object.

At any rate, in response to the definition that Humphrey and Laidlaw seek, one may point out that many events in secular life are completed—finishing a meal, a lecture, a holiday, a love affair—and that, as discrete, named entities, it is their "external" character that allows them to be reassimilated to the actor's intentions, attitudes, and beliefs. However, this criterion does not help one to identify "de-ritualization" as a secular mode. This is not to say that their definition is flawed; it is merely that a definition of ritual is not necessary for understanding the meaning of "ritual." The meaning of the term resides, as Wittgenstein says, in its various uses, not in a permanent fixed definition.[44]

Mauss was aware of this. "Prayer has a marvelous history," he wrote:

> Coming from the depths, it has gradually raised itself to the heights of religious life. Infinitely supple, it has taken the most varied forms, by turn adoring and coercive, humble and threatening, dry and full of imagery, immutable and variable, mechanical and mental. It has filled the most varied roles: here it is a brusque demand, there an order, elsewhere a contract, an act of faith, a confession, a supplication, an act of praise, a hosanna. Sometimes the same type of prayer has passed successively through all the vicissitudes: almost empty at first, one sort suddenly becomes full of meaning, while another, almost sublime to start with, gradually deteriorates into mechanical psalmody. . . . Prayer is speech. Now language is an activity that has an aim and effect: it is always, basically, an instrument of action. But it acts by expressing ideas and feelings that are externalized and given substance by words. To speak is both

to act and to think: that is why prayer gives rise to belief and ritual at the same time."[45]

In other words, Mauss stresses that prayer has several possible intentions, attitudes, and feelings, so in an important sense prayer is several kinds of acts.

Durkheim's conception of sociology (which Mauss develops) is not merely a claim about the ultimate nature of social reality (consisting of things) but an invitation to adopt a particular attitude in studying them "*as if* they were things," an attitude that focuses on their complex structures. Our attention, in other words, should be directed at the fact that, because following rules constitute rituals, the techniques being used in the practices provide the basis for objective judgment about what the point—the use—of each practice is. It is in that sense that intentional structures matter here and not simply in the trivial sense that the performance of ritual, like the performance of any act, is not accidental. What matters, however, is precisely to what extent and how the performer's intention, feeling, and attitude articulate a particular practice. This may include a casual or solemn style, an expression of particular hope or of a belief in its efficacy, a performance aimed at pleasing another or at cultivating a virtue.

Powers rightly qualifies the Humphrey–Laidlaw definition by pointing out that Islamic prayer assumes the centrality of two agents not allowed for in their approach (the agent who prays and God, in whose presence the prayer is performed) and that this relationship makes the worshiper's intention essential to the validity of the ritual. What needs to be noted, however, is that the anthropological definition leads to a conceptual separation between the formal behavior of ritual definable independently of the performer.

Part of the problem here is that both Powers and the anthropological study to which Powers turns for inspiration are concerned with "an ontology of ritual acts" (their being or essence) regardless of whether and, if so, how the acts may help to cultivate the subject performing them. According to the discursive tradition, the rules for prayer (*salāt*) are a means of getting nearer to God (*qurba*). In other words, *salāt* is not *simply* a communication addressed to God (it is distinguished, incidentally, from the *du'ā*, "supplication," appended at the end of the formal prayer) but part of an attempt to cultivate an appropriate attitude toward God in his presence. This formal awareness of nearness to God is also supplemented by a less formal—more everyday—awareness of friendship with God, especially (but not only) among Sufis, and referred to as *walīya*. Thus, in Islamic hagiography, the Prophet Abraham is known as "the bosom friend of God" (*khalīl allah*).[46] The language of prayer is thus connected, at various levels, to the hopes and desires of everyday life.

Although Powers points out that in Islamic ritual prayer (*salāt*) intention and will are together essential, he defines the latter as an internal force and the former as its directionality.[47] It is because will and intent are viewed as a conjoined internal cause that the ritual act is seen an external effect. What worries me about this way of looking at the problem is that the most important point of the prayer (the subject learning to articulate her faith) is missed, and the traditional norm being learned is confused with the experience of the performer—that is, with what she thinks the prayer means. The recited words and body movements in prayer aim not at creating a belief (an intellectual doctrine) but an attitude of reverence and a desire (intention) to get closer to God. I stress that I refer here not to the private experience of every performer but to the point of the prayer as stipulated by the discursive tradition.

Powers attributes a view, consistent with the anthropologists' definition, to Sherman Jackson's study of a thirteenth-century jurist from Egypt, Shihab al-Din al-Qaraf : "As a silent and internal phenomenon," Powers writes "this subjective element [viz., intention] is, by definition, unavailable for objective evaluation. One possible implication of this fact is reflected in Qarāfī, who argues on this basis that the *'ibādāt* [norms of worship] are not the business of the government. As Jackson shows, Qarāfī's view of *niyya* [intention] as a necessary and irreducibly subjective element of the *'ibādāt* serves his wider effort to establish the limits of legitimate state interference in religious practice."[48] And again a page later: "Given the general treatment of *niyya* [intention] in the *'ibādāt* as having no necessary connection to any outward, manifest indicants, it is simply not available for objective analysis. . . . Our discussion of *niyya* [intention] in the *'ibādāt* indicates that the jurists recognize the limits of their own ability to know the subjective state of others."[49] However, to the extent that government powers cannot determine what counts as genuine worship, I would argue that this is not because intention in prayer is essentially a subjective cause and therefore inaccessible but because intention is constitutive of ritual prayer and therefore not, as such, authoritatively translatable.

Actually Jackson does not say it is the impossibility of accessing the subjective element in prayer that limits government interference in religious practice; his argument, as I understand it, is that the absence of an established consensus on matters of worship among the learned limits the ability of government to define true worship.[50] In other words, what he points to is not psychological impossibility but grammatical impossibility, and it is on this basis that governmental authority (and, by implication, the authority of any other agency) is said to be limited in relation to the worshiper. This is consistent with the claim that intention is not, in fact, a purely subjective phenomenon but a publicly accessible construct—requiring the interpretation of words, behavior, and context—that together define its proper use. This not to say that there is no such thing as a private thought but that having thoughts and intentions is dependent on language as a social fact.

Powers needs to say (but doesn't) that it is wrong to talk about intention (*niyya*) as essentially an inner mental act separate from outer behavior when right intention is an aspect (what Wittgenstein would call an avowal) of the ritual act, something that makes it what it is. There is no question of legal invalidity; a court cannot pronounce a given act of prayer invalid on the grounds that the intention essential to it was absent. This is not, however, because only the performer really knows what the intention is but because performing prayer properly is a matter of learning to develop the attitude of reverence in the presence of God, and this implies in the life of a faithful Muslim. Of course the performance of prayer may occur in the presence of other persons—notably, in the Friday prayer and in the prayer over a dead body before its burial, where a congregation follows a prayer leader (*imām*)—but a parent teaching her child how to pray properly, how to recite and perform appropriate body movements, also urges him, directly and indirectly, how to develop a proper attitude; she does not say, "I can't do this because I can never know what his intention really is." (She knows when he is lying by paying attention to what he says and how.) Relatives, friends, and teachers, can access the intention of a worshiper because that is how appropriate intentions (and therefore proper ways of worshiping) are taught. The untranslatability of Qur'anic verses uttered in ritual prayer is not about inaccessibility of private thoughts but about the formation of a particular kind of ritual.

To repeat: if intention in Islamic worship is not the business of governors, this is not because it can never under any circumstances be accessed by other than the subject of intent but because according to shari'a texts, intention in worship is supposed to aim at forging the right relationship between the worshipper herself and her God—and this applies to all acts of worship, not only to the ritual of prayer (*salāt*). It applies, for example, to the solemnity of mandatory fasting (*sawm*) and to mandatory charity (*zakāt, sadaqa*), both being kinds of acts that may be possible to perform in a very casual manner.

The casual manner of abstaining from food and drink during the day throughout the month of Ramadan or of giving materially out of one's property to others are as much part of worship (*'ibāda*) as mandatory prayers are—their aim is, by repetition, to cultivate an appropriate attitude toward God, a relationship articulated by appropriate intention, thought, and feeling; they are not matters for a court to decide. Thus charity (*zakāt*) aims at transforming the giver and not the receiver in awareness of God's presence; it is not to be regarded as an expression of personal generosity for which the recipient is expected to be grateful or, for that matter, simply as the "right of God" (*haq allah*) but as a formal act of worship that is—given its significance for the worshipper—at once instrumental and expressive.

Incidentally, in a valuable historical study, Lena Salaymeh has recently argued that, in the early Islamic community, paying charity tax (*zakāt*) was an act "for-the-polity" that defined identity and not—as it became much later—simply an act "for-the-divine." Salaymeh is right to warn against anachronistic references to "belief" in this as in other contexts. Her insistence that the payment of tax to political authorities and not "belief" was crucial in the definition of the Muslim as a member of the commonwealth is therefore interesting.[51] But my discussion here is not concerned with the quasi-legal distinction between actions required by the state and those required by God.[52] I am concerned to understand whether and, if so, how an externally observable act such as mandatory charity (*zakāt*), like the act of mandatory prayer itself (*salāt*), can be realized through a discipline of feeling-will-attitude as an act of worship. My interest is not in the theological criteria for defining "the real Muslim" (let alone in describing his "real experience and belief") or in the political criteria for "belonging" to the earliest Muslim polity. It is simply that when *zakāt* is seen and treated essentially as a mode of social redistribution, when it no longer aspires to be part of an attitude in confronting God, "charity" becomes a secular concept that is therefore derivualized.[3] And central to that understanding is the view that *irāda* (will/intention) is not the mental cause of an act but in itself constitutive of an act of worship and, as such, helping to articulate not only worship but also the worshiper.

Regarding the accessibility of will/intention, it may be noted that in interpersonal relations such as divorce and commercial dealings (issues dealt with in the second half of Powers' book), intention *is* accessible—it is determined by a judge in court by reference to admissible forms of evidence. In other words, where rights and duties, and conflicting claims based on them, have to be decided on, the grammar of intention/will is different from the grammar in prayer. It is certainly not inaccessible because it is subjective.

Of course, even in mandatory acts of worship more than one intention may be at work. For example, the performance of prayer may, in addition to performing one's religious duties, also be a way of pleasing one's parents, although that assimilates the sense of intended action to the consequences foreseen by the actor rather than to the essential articulation of the prayer itself—and such intentions may or may not vitiate it.

The distinction between these two senses is crucial for virtue ethics because it might allow one to justify any action, however reprehensible, by a process of individual thought that redirects intention. In the domains of ethics and politics—and political ethics—the result of the understanding intentionality as a private mental event has, Elizabeth Anscombe argued, been disastrous. "From the seventeenth century till now," she writes,

> what may be called Cartesian psychology has dominated the thought of philosophers and theologians. According to this psychology, an intention was an interior act of the mind which could be produced at will. Now if intention is all important—as it is—in determining the goodness or badness of an action, then, on this theory of what intention is, a

marvelous way offered itself of making any action lawful. You only had to "direct your intention" in a suitable way. In practice, this means making a little speech to yourself: "What I mean to be doing is. . . ."[54]

And she concludes with reference to the conduct of war: "The same doctrine is used to prevent any doubts about the obliteration bombing of a city. The devout Catholic bomber secures by a 'direction of intention' that any shedding of innocent blood that occurs is 'accidental.' . . . It is nonsense to pretend that you do not intend to do what is the means you take to your chosen end. Otherwise there is absolutely no substance to the Pauline teaching that we may not do evil that good may come."[55]

Intention/desire that is identified by the manuals are essential to the structuration of the act of prayer, making it at once instrumental (an act with an aim) and expressive (of a desire). Of course, one can intentionally deceive others, but such deception is parasitic on acts (words, behavior, etc.) that are publicly understandable and accessible; and in acts of prayer, the deception can be directed only at other human persons, not at God, who is assumed by believers to be incapable of being deceived: one cannot therefore deceive *in* prayer, but one can fail to have the appropriate intention.

There are, in fact, different ways that intentions have been identified in history: for example, in medieval Christian confession of the flesh and in Freudian psychoanalysis, in torture both medieval and modern, and in modern law's distinction between acts that are "intentional" and "reckless" as well as in personal relations such as between a parent and a child or between lovers. In all these cases the truth *can* be accessed by resorting to distinctive theories and techniques and by close attention to silences and emphasis in language. To the extent that intention articulates prayer, it is neither essentially private nor strictly speaking public. It is an embodied practice—at once oriented toward the deity and using socially accessible criteria that enable proper learning and judgment. Intention is not, therefore, to be confused with a private thought (a private meaning), although Powers appears to do so. As Wittgenstein pointed out. "'obeying a rule' is a practice. And to *think* one is obeying a rule is not to obey a rule. Hence it is not possible to obey a rule 'privately': otherwise thinking one was obeying a rule would be the same thing as obeying it."[56] Intention is not a kind of privately apprehended rule that is subjectively put into action and therefore inaccessible to the state.

IX

The idea that "will" inhabits an internal space of absolute freedom and "intent" gives it direction is a relatively recent one that posits an opposition between reason and affect, between acts that express and acts that bring something about as fundamental.[57] In an older understanding, "will" and "intention" help to constitute particular actions, each shaped by the agent's feeling or passion that are reflected in the way he or she behaves and talks in public. Will, intention, and desire are regarded as aspects of action, not as its cause. When an observer identifies someone's behavior as reverential (or courageous or vindictive), it is because something specific is articulated in discourse and action, not because something in the actor's mind ("intention") precedes and brings it about.

Of course, the old vocabulary has not been discarded; it has been made available in addition to the new when social purposes require it. Thus, when the white American Stephen Paddock carried out his massacre in Las Vegas, it was described as the act of someone "mentally disturbed," and because he killed himself, the question of legal responsibility didn't formally arise; the search for an apparently motiveless killing led to postmortem studies of the killer's brain.[58] On the other hand, when the Uzbek immigrant Sayfullo

Saipov deliberately ran over and killed a number of people on a side-walk in New York, he was heard to shout "Allahu Akbar!" ("God is Great!") shortly before being shot; he was taken to be a terrorist because his outburst proved he was "inspired by ISIS." This proved his intention and indicated that he had acted freely and willfully and was therefore responsible for his act.[59]

The tendency, found in much theorizing, to speak of human intention and will as essentially internal phenomena, as causally prior to behavior and therefore not directly accessible, also promotes a language of event causation that incidentally competes with a language of agent responsibility, with the former based on the physical laws of an impersonal universe and the latter on freedom of the will, on a self whose essence is internally located and therefore prior to spoken words and observable actions. In the classical view as well as in the view of Ghazālī, passion and will, intention and desire, body and mind articulate an action that is virtuous or vicious, and that is why one is responsible for them.

There is, of course, no single moment of origin for such a momentous historical change in our understanding of will and intention, especially given the continuous arguments over the meaning and reality of "causality" since early modernity, but historians of ideas point to seventeenth-century philosophers such as René Descartes as having contributed to this major shift from ancient usage. Thus, the new cosmology that emerged in seventeenth-century Europe rendered the human body part of the mechanical world and thus "alien" to the self and the object of technological mastery, like everything in the material world. For early thinkers such as Stoics and Epicureans, the will could not be reduced to a mediated physical event but was regarded as a way of signifying the adoption of a favorable attitude toward a particular objective.[60]

My point here is simply that the shift to a language for describing the psychological dynamics of internal cause and effect is one of the moments at which the space for resorting to what people would call "secular explanations of action" is enlarged. An interesting example of this shift is to be found in the history of the insanity defense in the secular formalities of law courts. From the beginning of the eighteenth century to about the middle of the nineteenth, the concept of "knowing right from wrong," rooted in a free "conscience" and a free "will," was established in Anglo-American law. Together with the somewhat later notion of "mental disease," a notion based on material determinism, and with other forms of what came to be described as "the impairment of intent," it became a precondition for a full account of intent as "willful"—and therefore of attributing criminal liability to an agent. In other words, modern law does not consider "intent" to be inaccessible, but in order to access it, the courts have to call on the assistance of the secular discipline of psychiatry to explain whether—and if so, to what extent—will and intention, as internal causal functions, are impaired and therefore liability diminished. By the middle of the twentieth century, psychiatric and even psychoanalytic theories of intentionality in criminal behavior had become virtually standard.[61]

The modern individual supposedly demonstrates his personal freedom (his free will) not only by his ability to direct the act in any direction he wishes but also by claiming to justify the embodied act that results through an internal act of translation and redescription. This concept of personal freedom has no need of tradition.

X

When Sanneh writes "language is the intimate, articulate expression of culture," he implies—although he does not make this explicit—that changes in the uses of language are intimately connected to changes in ways of life. Change in the use of such terms as "will" points to another way in which people's relationships and understanding of one another also changes. Therefore, when language is changed to accommodate a modern Christian vision of life, it changes not only the way of life but also the body and its senses. One crucial aspect of that is the distinction between a "real" self (subjectivity) and the self that is conventional—the "apparent" self. Another is the sharp distinction between the materiality of the body and the meaning-producing mind.

The language of the "real" self and its external appearance is itself closely connected to sixteenth- and seventeenth-century reforms in European Christianity that afforded possibilities for secular developments. From the sixteenth century on, after the upheavals of the Reformation, liturgy and ritual generally were criticized and attacked with the aim of eliminating what came to be regarded as superstition, and to revise the content of liturgy in accordance with new theological doctrines. By the end of the eighteenth century, a very different attitude to ritual had crystallized, in which spontaneity was highly valued, not only in religious experience and poetry but also in interpersonal relations and consumer desire. In her rich account of sentiment and secularism from John Bunyan in the sixteenth century to William Wordsworth in the late eighteenth, Lori Branch asks how and why the popular conception of poetry shifted from ritual repetition and communal performance to the outpouring of emotional sincerity. "How was it," she writes, "that the history of Christian worship . . . an evolving millennium-and-a-half-long liturgical tradition, suddenly witnessed a principled defense of the effusions of free prayer that lives on in today's televangelism and megachurches?"[62] She emphasizes that this question can't be answered in any simple fashion by identifying a single origin, and she recounts instead the extended debates and evolving discourses through which the transformation occurred.

In valuing spontaneity, Branch notes, the process of thought removes religion from the tradition within which the self is developed—and thus also from belief as action and social relationship—and roots it in an inner psychological state. She notes, however, "Ritual and belief do not vanish in the imagined secular space of spontaneous responses, but crucially are naturalized and made invisible, less and less subject to resistant behaviors and credible reimagining."[63] That's to say, new rituals are invented but not thought of as "ritual"—most prominent among them being the compulsiveness of "free prayer" itself, together with the overriding emphasis on self-scrutiny and the formalized expressions of joy and weeping. But because the correct performance of prescribed ritual is easy to identify whereas the identification of true belief in free prayer is not, anxiety about authenticity is inevitably generated. A notable accompaniment to this new form of religiosity was the production of guidebooks to spontaneous prayer that encouraged believers to compile phrases from scripture that could be recited in moments of crippling doubt and inability to pray. "Followed carefully," she writes, "the story of spontaneity ultimately questions generally assumed distinctions between the secular and religious subjects while highlighting their unnoticed differences, and ultimately suggests the startling question of whether the idea of a secular space devoid of uncertainty and therefore of the vulnerability of belief is not the constitutive (and gendered) fantasy both of Enlightenment, and of the modern forms of religion it generates."[64] This statement seems to me particularly perceptive in its focus on a new kind of "belief" driven by an obsession with authenticity.

XI

But it might be objected at this point: Isn't authenticity (the sense of something being true or genuine by virtue of its origin) precisely an obsession also of tradition? And isn't that precisely the point of the important historical critiques that focus on "the invention of tradition?"[65]

So perhaps I should say a few words finally about my use of the term "discursive tradition": It is intended to focus on the ways language directs, justifies, and permeates the senses of the living body through the repeated performance of virtuous action, thought, and feeling (what Ghazālī called "exercising the soul"). In an important sense, tradition links the dead to the living. But discursive tradition produces statements about how practical aspects of the past can or cannot be reproduced in the present. One might think this is a concern with authenticity, but the authenticity of a traditional practice is not the same as the authenticity of an identity that exercises "free will." In the former, it relates to questions about time: about whether what is essential to the tradition is located at once in the past and the present, whether something in the tradition still properly belongs to it. In the latter, it is a matter of asserting who the real agent is. To invoke the authority of the past is a matter of interpretation, of translating the past into the present, which inevitably involves the unique potentialities and demands of the present. Conversely, arguments over whether something belongs to the discursive tradition (for example, whether the modern state is or is not compatible with Islamic tradition) have different intellectual and practical implications for someone who takes part in it as a member of the tradition as opposed to someone who relates to it as an "objective construct" with no immediate significance for his life. How the speaker relates to the audience of an argument is part of its sense—by which I do not mean that those who are not committed to a discursive tradition cannot criticize it.

In my usage, discursive tradition is not a synonym for religion or for the absence of secular freedom. It signals an attempt to engage with the multiple temporalities of those who aspire to a shared inheritance—as well as those who reject it. Discursivity—the cold or hot use of language and its receptivity by the senses—may be rooted in a sense of unease about disjunctions between what one believes to be a traditional norm and how one lives in the present. At that level there is no inside and outside, there is only a tension of which one has become conscious and that demands a resolution. The history of reform of discursive tradition is precisely a matter of some Muslims trying to persuade others that what was hitherto thought to be "outside" is really "inside"—at least that it has always been potentially part of it. This is usually done by resort to interpretations of what was said and done by authoritative sources (by communities of practice extending over time) in the tradition's history, starting with the Qur'an and the Sunnah (tradition) of the Prophet Muhammad, to argue for the contingency (and therefore replaceability) of a given practice or doctrine in order to save the tradition's essence. A tradition is a set of aspirations, sensibilities, felt obligations, and relationships of subjects who live and move in the multiple times of a common world—whence the possibilities for disagreement.

Arguably, neither "authenticity" nor "unquestioning obedience" belong to tradition as I use the term because and to the extent that they imply conscious judgment. Living a tradition is not, strictly speaking, a matter of justifying obedience to another person by reference to an intellectually recognized authority but of learning to live without justification. The language of tradition is therefore not the language of the state in so far as the law, whether issued or authorized by the state, demands obedience.

Law is connected to discursive tradition when it demands the defense or restoration of modes of behavior and relationship specified either by custom or by a written rule. But discursive tradition is not itself law: Shari'a (derived fundamentally from the Qur'an and the Prophet's tradition) is often referred to as a legal tradition, as the central inheritance of Islamic life. But it is different from "law" as understood and practiced in modern society. Thus, in a recent article on Islamic law as tradition, Ahmed Fekry Ibrahim correctly emphasizes that

Islamic law (sharia) is different from other legal systems in that it includes ritual and ethical rules, such as etiquette, hygiene, and prayer. Although the coercive power of the state is employed to ensure observance of many aspects of the law, the violation of some ritual and ethical rules does not carry any punitive measures, and therefore a primary concern of Islamic law is care of the self. Even the strictly punitive, legal aspects of Islamic law to be found, for instance, in criminal law carry eschatological consequences that are, for some Muslims, more serious than their worldly consequences.[66]

The shari'a is not, however, merely *more* than the operation of modern secular law simply because it includes rules of worship and because—for pious believers—punishment in the life to come for violating norms is more important than its worldly consequences. It is *different* because epistemological questions concerning the foundational understanding of shari'a norms (*usūl al-fiqh*) are central to the ways they articulate the care of the soul. Thus, unlike modern law (for whom the fundamental questions of legitimacy are institutional, for example, between common law and statute), for *fiqh* the validity of norms, being essentially epistemological, depends on the cognate disciplines of theology and grammar.[67]

What I call discursive tradition focuses, therefore, not on the definition of meanings but, in an important sense, on the behavioral customs and the sensibilities they teach and regulate in the process of disciplining the soul; it is to this that the act of defining or justifying concepts is directed. As the highly influential medieval theologian Ibn Taymiyya argued in his famous critique of Greek logic, the members of different professions, whether intellectual or practical, do not need to have their concepts (*tasawwurāt*) abstracted, defined, and reified so long as they know how to do and say what is appropriate to their profession.[68] The implication here is that tradition for each of these professions is not merely a chain of ideas to be abstracted and applied correctly but contextually embedded practices that are learned and that come to be inhabited in communities over time—practices that include verbal conventions (*'urf qawli*) and behavioral customs (*'urf 'amali*). The proper performance of those practices depends crucially not on rules and abstract concepts (products of Reason) but on learning how to do something and on a community that can confirm that it is properly done (reasoning in context). Language is never merely a means of communication, nor is communication—or any other "function," for that matter—essential to language.

As Ibn Taymiyya suggests, the plausibility of arguments itself depends crucially on the sensibilities, habits, and relationships that articulate individuals—and therefore on what makes sense to them in their lives—and not on a universalizing logic. When reform is felt to be necessary, there is an assumption, explicit or implicit, that the tradition's essence—what is perceived by those who inhabit it to be essential—is not to be changed but defended through interpretation and translation. One might say that tradition always carries the time in which declarations about what is "essential" to a religion are made and secured. The "essence" is not neutrally determinable because it is subject to argument. A living tradition is not merely capable of containing conflict and disagreement; the search for what is essential itself provokes argument. A concern with "essence" is therefore not quite the same as a concern with authenticity.

And yet the call for reform in order to adjust to "the world as it really is" inevitably encounters the question as to what drives that call. Is the desire for reform actuated by thoughts of worldly benefit? Or does it issue from a wish to prevent the tradition from becoming irrelevant in the world? Whatever the motive—and of course there are many motives for advocating change or resisting it—some rightly argue that the call for adjusting to "the real world," whether it includes the past or not, is never in itself the measure of rational action.

In short, there is no irreconcilable opposition between tradition and genealogy, between what is contingent and what is essential, between critique and exercise of the soul. The very attempt to "purify tradition" draws on genealogical arguments, points to contingencies, and draws on ambiguities that emerge over time. Genealogical critique is not a rejection of *all* grounding as it is sometimes alleged; its ground is "this moment," the place in which one thinks, acts, and lives and from which one regards past and future. In time, attentiveness to reason and proper repetition transforms the subject's willfulness or refractoriness (*'isyān*) into virtuous action guided and informed by the language of tradition—which also belongs to this moment. Spontaneity is an act that claims truthfulness merely on the grounds that it emerges from the "real" individual, and it stands opposed, in that sense, to the discipline of tradition.

XII

"Language" is not separable from "the message" conveyed in it, and the message is not simply cognitive. As Wittgenstein says, don't look for the meaning (of an enunciation) look to its use. That is to say, not only to how the subject uses language but also to how language uses him or her. Contrary to many linguists, I have suggested that there is no "primary purpose" of language. Translating the Qur'anic vision into the sensible body (and especially as it is enunciated in ritual prayer) is made possible by the language of the Qur'an as well as by supplementary discourses that seek to teach certain virtues central to it, and the primary purpose of Qur'anic language here is not simply to communicate but to model—with the help of relatives, friends, and teachers—a process in which communication is, of course, an element but an element that cannot be "abstracted." To those like Lamin Sanneh and Willard Oxtoby, who point out that Christian scriptures have, almost uniquely, been translated into numerous languages for liturgical purposes, the thought may be offered that the scriptures become less and less relevant to how Christians actually live.[69] At any rate, it is almost impossible to say what kind of life people are actually living simply on the basis of their declared Christian beliefs.

One might suppose that, unlike natural languages, the language of numbers is independent of the way of life in which it is used because it is abstract, and that this is precisely the reason for its great success in the realm of scientific knowledge. But that language is not simply integral to modern collective life; it is crucial in shaping its character. To abstract is itself an act. Central to that abstract language, including probability theory, is that it enables a move from a reading of the world as a display of signs (including the distinction between an "authentic" self and its "public" appearance) to reconstructing the world in which the subject lives—remaking it through the modern state and advanced capitalism and the science and technology on which both depend. In an important sense, the primary language of secular reason that employs numbers requires inattention to the world from which it has been abstracted. Such reason deals with risk not simply as a danger but as an opportunity for the continuous increase of knowledge, wealth, and power.

3

Masks, Security, and the Language of Numbers

In this final chapter I explore certain aspects of translation, both verbal and numerical, relating to the modern nation-state. I turn first to some contemporary ethnographers and sociologists who have written about ritual as a formal expression of the distinction between a private, authentic self and the self's publicly presented behavior, a distinction that depends crucially on the presentation and reading of masks as signs. Next, I go on to trace masking and the reading of masks as a pivotal feature of princely status in early modernity and its subsequent role in modern state power. This leads me to a discussion of suspicion and paranoia in modern society and from there to a particular kind of paranoia: the search for signs of political treason regarded by government as a betrayal of nation-state solidarity because it is the elected government and not "the people" that directly exercises state power and defends the nation's solidarity. But the power of the modern state depends on using a distinctive language the language of numbers. This is exemplified in a crucial modality of solidarity in the modern nation-state: namely, insurance. I conclude by examining the most important preoccupation with numbers in the democratic nation-state: the distinction between the demographic majority and the demographic minority, the nation-state being assumed to belong more to the former than to the latter. This concern with whom the nation-state essentially belongs to, a concern with its essential character, is also expressed in a discourse that translates the nation's origins in ways that support the state's claims.

At the very end I propose that we are witnessing today the beginnings of an alarming development that goes beyond the nation-state: life rendered as signs—that is, as computable and translatable information.

I

It was Marcel Mauss's famous last essay, "A Category of the Human Mind: The Notion of Person; the Notion of Self," that first problematized that category in anthropology.[1] Its purpose was to alert scholars to the fact that the philosophical use of the word "self" (*moi*)—that is, of the idea of "the self"—and derived ideas such as "the cult of the self," "self-respect," and "respect of others" (what we now call respecting their "dignity") were all very recent. Mauss traces the idea of *person* from classical Latin, where it meant "a mask" that was at once a screen of reality and an expression of passion, through the medieval Christian notion, where it acquired a metaphysical dimension (the unity of the three persons of the Trinity, and of the two natures of Christ) to our modern notion (Locke's legal person, the continuous subject of responsibility). Mauss claims that the Christian idea of person is still the one that underlies our secular category of the self today. But I want to suggest that the Roman mask (what Mauss identifies as "a tragic mask, a ritual mask, and the ancestral mask") is more important for much of our modern life and politics than he seems to assume. If the self is thought of as autonomous and naturally self-interested, one can understand why a mask offers itself as a useful protection and negotiating aid in an uncertain—and possibly devious—world. But for those who encounter it, a mask has to be read, translated, and responded to appropriately.

The mask is part of the genealogy of "the person" and therefore stands for dualities that replicate aspects of the inner and the outer, a topic of central concern to much modern philosophy: mind and body (the former directly accessible only to the subject), the individual and the relational (the former as agent, the latter as social constraint or process of negotiation), the private and the public (each standing for different political, moral, and epistemological positions).[2] Among anthropologists, these and other dualities have played an important part in the theorization of ritual and culture and in the practice of translation generally.

Wittgenstein's well-known claim that meaning is public (often misunderstood as a kind of behaviorism) has a resonance for many anthropologists.[3] People who know his work will recognize that I have used his insights to discuss the question of intention in the previous chapter. However, a more important issue that Wittgenstein opens up for anthropology is that not everything in life is to be interpreted. Interpretation (or "translation"), says Wittgenstein, is the process of substituting one formulation for another. The hermeneutical exercise of interpretation and translation deal, as Jakobson also reminded us, in signs. If "culture" is regarded as a space of meaningful signs instead of as inherited ways of learning to do things, then the life studied by the ethnographer comes to be regarded as a kind of text to be interpreted and translated. Thus Clifford Geertz writes in a well-known essay: "Doing ethnography is like trying to read (in the sense of 'construct a reading of') a manuscript—foreign, faded, full of ellipses, incoherencies, suspicious emendations, and tendentious commentaries, but written not in conventionalized graphs of sound but in transient examples of shaped behavior."[4] As indicated in previous chapters, I regard this view as highly problematical.

II

In a number of his writings, Maurice Bloch has argued that discursive conventions mask forms of social subjection, that when children are taught to be polite and respectful, when they learn conventional manners (whether in Madagascar, where Bloch conducted his ethnographic fieldwork, or in England, where he lived and taught) they are in effect being subjected to constraint.[5] And so the politeness that adults display on formal political occasions as well as in the course of everyday intercourse is really an instance of the exercise of social power through the skillful use of what are in effect masks. The thought here is that convention coerces a *real* self into behaving inauthentically.[6] This enables Bloch to represent formalization on a single continuum of coercion, at one extreme of which is religious ritual and at the other secular freedom.[7] These modes of the self, ranging from the most dominated to the most spontaneous, enable one to understand the secularization of ritual because ritual shares something with convention—namely, identifiability and repeatability. According to Bloch, it is precisely through formalization that coercion is exercised: "formalised language, the language of traditional authority," he writes, "is an impoverished language; a language where many of the options at all levels are abandoned so that choice of form, of style, of words and of syntax, is less than in ordinary language."[8] One obvious difficulty with this claim is that if it applies to *anyone* who uses formal language—or performs a ritual—the distinction between coercer and coerced cannot then be made on that basis alone.[9] In political coercion, what matters more than *what* is said and *how* it is said is *who* speaks *to whom* and in *what context*. Whether in the peasant society of Madagascar or in English industrial society, the one who coerces is the one who commands more resources and uses them to advance particular objectives against the wishes of others. If this view of coercion is accepted, it may still be possible to argue that, although ritualization may not be directly coercive, it may nevertheless hide coercion.

But it is not essential to see ritualization this way. Where ritual primarily contributes to making the self, to forming as well as expressing it and not merely to hiding its "true meaning," there our concepts of ritualization, of time, and of the self can be quite different. What the sensible body learns to say and do in that context is part of the self's potentiality—its ability to obey and to command, to adapt and to stand firm, to please and to offend. In other words, the achievement of ritualized practice is itself essential to what the self becomes, helping to form or to deform it.

Maurice Bloch assumes that in order to understand the activity of agents, their behavior should be conceptually abstracted from an autonomous and freely willing self (the ability to determine for oneself is, after all, what makes one free), and that when behavior and language are "ritualized" (i.e. expressed punctiliously in accordance with conventions), they perform significant social functions by repressing individuality. Adam Seligman, in his more interesting text, argues for ritual (socially prescribed words, gestures, etc.) as meliorative, but he also works from the idea that there is a private language and self quite independent of public language and behavior.[10] He sees ritual and sincerity as two ideal types of articulated experience, action, and understanding in different societies as well as in the different domains of one society. His claim is that ritual creates an "as if" or "could be," universe, thereby helping to make a shared social world. This shared world is expressed in sacred as well as profane sectors of social life. "Ritual and ritualistic behavior," Seligman writes, "are not so much events as ways of negotiating our very existence in the world. . . . Whenever the expressions 'please' and 'thank you' are used, when we ask a casual acquaintance, 'How are you?' both knowing in advance that we do not really expect an honest answer (which would be disastrous), we are enacting a crucial ritual for the maintenance of our shared social world."[11] Ritual, in this sense, conveys a message independent of the essential identity of the self that performs it, translating an uncertain world of mutually opaque individuals into a coherent society. Seligman and his coauthors contrast this kind of conventional interaction and the translations underpinning it with sincerity, which they see as projecting an "as is" vision of reality that is unambiguous and that therefore promotes "fundamentalist" belief (that is, arrogant certainty). This is an arresting way of conceptualizing ritual, although it is not clear why sincerity ("I really mean what I say") is regarded as incompatible with uncertainty: Can't one be sincere in confessing that one has doubts?

The world we live in is full of risks.[12] Yet the conventional rules that are being offered by some institutions as a way of negotiating our collective existence—in the form of everyday politesse, or of national ceremonial, or of the etiquette of war—are unable to address the multiple crises of our world. It is neither the religious language of divine texts nor the secular language of aesthetic experience but the language of quantification, abstraction, and calculation (that is, mathematics applied to human activity as well as to the "natural world" in which it takes place) that now seeks to resolve the major uncertainties of collective life.[13] Whether that language is adequate for the predicament it has helped to create is a moot question.

But I want to elaborate a little on the modern perception of the self that underlies much of what one might call everyday politics by reference to Erving Goffman's celebrated study, *The Presentation of Self in Everyday Life*, published in 1956.[14] Goffman came out of the Chicago urban sociology school, but this book became much more influential than anything published by his mentors and colleagues in Chicago sociology, partly because it reinforced and supplied an original theoretical dimension to urban ethnography. Goffman describes his approach in that book as dramaturgical, as an analysis of interpersonal interaction within delimited spaces, of actors playing roles intended to secure strategic advantage, of selves separate from publicly recognizable enactments. In any given situation, Goffman argues, every individual attempts to control others by controlling the impression he makes on them. He does this by trying to suppress his feelings and present a view of himself to others that accords with his objectives in the particular situation.[15]

> Regardless of the particular objective which the individual has in mind and of his motive for having this objective, it will be in his interests to control the conduct of the others, especially their responsive treatment of him. This control is achieved largely by influencing the definition of the situation which the others come to formulate, and he can influence this definition by expressing himself in such a way as to give them the kind of impression that will lead them to act voluntarily in accordance with his own plan.[16]

In the process of face-to-face interaction, there are situations in which first impressions are critical. Goffman cites a teacher talking about the importance of first impressions presented to school pupils: "You can't ever let them get the upper hand on you or you're through. So I start out tough. The first day I get a new class in, I let them know who's boss. . . . You've got to start off tough, then you can ease up as you go along. If you start out easy-going, when you try to get tough, they'll just look at you and laugh."[17] Whether it is a teacher on her first day in class or an attendant in a mental institution encountering a new patient, Goffman stresses the importance of presenting an authoritative persona in encountering weaker or personally disoriented and socially disturbing individuals. The actor's body-voice is the medium; the presentation is the message. The persona represented is not merely a personal presentation; it helps to construct a certain kind of social order.

A decade after Goffman's famous book, Alvin Gouldner launched an attack against it in his *The Coming Crisis of Western Sociology*. In place of Goffman's subtle analyses of practical rules for strategic face-to-face interaction, Gouldner offers a critical analysis of class ideology. He believes that Goffman's world view marks a radical change in the world, "from men capable of moral indignation to 'merchants of morality'; from men of self-absorbed Calvinist conscience to gamesmen adroitly making their moves, not in accord with inward consultation, but in shrewd anticipation of the other's countermove; . . . from the criticism of 'insincerity' to the acceptance that all is insincerity."[18] Goffman's theory, says Gouldner, is that behavior that appears spontaneous is really a calculated show. Gouldner's fundamental argument is that Goffman's sociology is an ideological expression of the world in which the educated middle classes in the West now live, a world experienced in a new way, giving rise to new conceptions of "reality" through affects that undermine what was once their living tradition. The middle classes now live in a world of uncertainty that they cannot control. Written before neoliberalism became the official ideology of most governments, Gouldner's book regards the irrationalities of modern political economy as intrinsic to both civil society and the state, and attributes the attenuation of public authority and political legitimacy to the underlying deceptions of civil society and the state.

Gouldner's warning against the dismissal of sincerity seems to me persuasive, as does his protest against the substitution of "gamesmanship" for morality—although I would say, following Quentin Skinner's comment on Leo Strauss, that what we have here is not an absence of morality but a different conception of (attitude toward) morality.[19] What concerns me most is that Gouldner doesn't address directly the fact that it is the systematic separation of the self from its publicly observable behavior that enables these attitudes—and what that separation might mean for a national politics. It is therefore worth reminding ourselves of a European history of the self beginning prior to the flowering of bourgeois society. So here is a brief, unavoidably incomplete sketch.

III

The desire for a secure and autonomous self, an authentic self that is free to perform (or not perform) rituals has a well-known religious history, but that is only part of the story. I say "only part of the story" because that view of the self has emerged in close connection with complex political, economic, and social forces.

As European societies became increasingly marketized and wealthy—in part by pillaging the world—as opportunities for social mobility multiplied, as individuals found themselves confronting possible opponents and allies, behavior for a *successful* self came to be theorized. Texts, produced for the literate classes, discussed the value and the danger of opportunistic behavior (later known as "entrepreneurship"). When conventional behavior is seen as disconnected from the self and acquires the status of a tactic, there is a tendency to present theories of self-interest and theories of public good as mutually compatible.

Here is one of the most famous Renaissance writers in the mirror-for-princes tradition:

A man who wishes to make a profession of goodness in everything must necessarily come to grief among so many who are not good. Therefore it is necessary for a prince, who wishes to maintain himself, to learn how not to be good, and to use this knowledge and not use it, according to the necessity of the case. . . . A prince must take great care that nothing goes out of his mouth which is not full of [virtue], and, to see and hear him, he should seem to be all mercy, faith, integrity, humanity, and religion. And nothing is more necessary than to seem to have this last quality, for men in general judge more by the eyes than by the hands, for everyone can see, but very few have to feel.[20] Everybody sees what you appear to be, few feel what you are, and those few will not dare to oppose themselves to the many, who have the majesty of the state to defend them.[21]

Niccolò Machiavelli's advice to the prince is that he wear a mask to guard and further his sovereignty—a mask that doesn't merely hide his real intent and feeling but presents conventionally recognizable behavior to an audience to achieve a desired result: that is to say, presenting an *image* of feelings and intentions is important not in what it does to the agent but in how it works on viewers. The mask as a presentation of self is an instrument, a sign of the ambiguous qualities that are put in play when sovereignty, personal and political, is to be defended or enhanced.

In his magnum opus on early modern European political thought, Quentin Skinner defends Machiavelli against the many moralistic judgments that have been made about him—such as that of Leo Strauss who "insists in his *Thoughts on Machiavelli* that the doctrines of *The Prince* are simply 'immoral and irreligious,' and that their author can only be characterized as 'a teacher of evil.'"[22] Skinner insists that such views

embody a misunderstanding of the relationship between his outlook and that of his contemporaries. Machiavelli and the more conventional writers on princely government are in complete agreement . . . about the nature of the goals which princes ought to pursue. As Machiavelli repeatedly affirms, their aim should be to "maintain their state," to "achieve great things" and to seek for the highest goals of honour, glory and fame. . . . The crucial difference between Machiavelli and his contemporaries lies in the nature of the methods they took to be appropriate for the attainment of these ends. . . . Thus the difference between Machiavelli and his contemporaries can- not adequately be characterized as a difference between a moral view of politics and a view of politics divorced from morality. The essential contrast is rather between two differ- ent moralities—two rival and incompatible accounts of what ought ultimately to be done.[23]

Skinner is right, of course, about there being two conceptions of morality here, but I would put the contrast slightly differently: Translated into twentieth-century liberal morality, one might say that Machiavelli is urging the sovereign to be *sensible about goodness.* Achievability and efficiency are at least as important as the virtue of honor when moral behavior is expected of a person in charge of the state, and, by extension, of anyone entering the domain of pol- itics. What matters ultimately for the modern state (a comprehen- sive frame of modern life) is responsibility for maintaining and enhancing its power and reputation. For this, sound calculation and strategizing by both the state and private corporations are essen- tial. Where the secular aims of politics are ultimately honorable, moral arguments about means should not be allowed to threaten them. The protoliberal reasoning here is that precisely because the ultimate political aims are honorable, acts essential to furthering and maintaining them are ethically acceptable even if they have unintended consequences that would otherwise deserve moral con- demnation. Thus, one is morally responsible for the ultimate aim but not for choosing the means to achieve it.

   Appeals to self-interest were at once the conceptual precondi- tion and discursive consequence not only of political sovereignty that Machiavelli speaks of but also of market society that renders self-interest a central virtue. Faith that once referred to the value of trust in a relationship was now coming to be emphasized as a state of mind and as a synonym for religious authority that, incidentally, was rendered more precarious than ever when confronted—as it increasingly was—by the authority of natural science and required to defend itself in secular language. Discipline of the self is not done away with in this newly emerging world: when it is not a requirement of "objective knowledge" it is increasingly posed as an aesthetic task, as the cultivation of a freely choosing agent, whose free will is typically expressed in the spontaneous purchase of goods for sale and in the employment of political strategies—including standing as and voting for candidates.[24] Hence, self-interest was also accompanied by the notion of disinterest—in the early modern sense of "impartiality"—a virtue to be cultivated in government, in the law, and above all in the pursuit of science. To the extent that disinterest was opposed to self-interest, public debates over the matter drew support from both religious and nonreligious sides: skeptics as well as believers were to be found on both sides of the argument.

The cultivation of spontaneity that I mentioned in the previous chapter helped to promote the literary, religious, aesthetic movement later called Romanticism, expressed in and through a particular kind of self. But one result of the obsession with authenticity was continual individual anxiety about whether prayer or consumer satisfaction, poetic expression or social behavior, was authentic or not.[25] Care of the self is of course as much a part of modern liberal society as of premodern institutions although its general regulators now tend to be not "religious thought and practice" but varying combinations of the market, the nation-state, and technology.

Constituted through dramas of manipulative power, at once psychological, political, and economic, the Renaissance self now required more than ever the maintenance and extension of a moral distance between public behavior and private virtue. The dramas of power composed by historians and playwrights of the Renaissance gain in credibility because of the play between inner thought and outer behavior that they describe. But it was the product, too, of a radical reconceptualization of ritualized behavior as a presentation to be read by others. In the seventeenth century, it was precisely the discourse of the private self separate from the publicly displayable figure, of "genuine" Christian commitment separate from the duties of civic office, that enabled a relaxation of hostilities between Catholic and Protestant princes at the termination of the Thirty Years' War.

As European empires and settlements took over much of the world, a concept of "religion" began to crystallize—a concept of something at once universal, individual, and plural—through which the possibility was increasingly opened up of deploying ritualization (repetition, formalization, tradition) in games of power. In a developing culture that located the agent in a natural world of unchanging laws and that sometimes encouraged skepticism, the notion of disinterest was at once impugned and valorized—impugned because it seemed to indicate a lack of compassion where that was conventionally expected, and valorized because the self was required to abstract itself in the pursuit of scientific knowledge—the most prestigious form of knowledge in modernity. (Much later, closer to our own time, both self-interest and disinterest were absorbed into the institutionalization of suspicion and risk—a topic to which I turn below.)

Of course, representational behavior was involved not only in power play, and of course deception was not absent prior to the modern epoch. My point is simply that the separation of the "true" self from its action, behavior, way of living, was in great measure a consequence of religious reforms in early modernity. Interestingly, this kind of valorization of the individual was at first also seen as passionate—as passive—that allowed divine grace to enter. To the extent that it was conceived of as passive, the self was also seen as capable of receiving a transcendental force within and thus of acting disinterestedly in its name. So the skeptical argument that all human action is naturally self-interested was (and has been) evaded by the claim that the passionate self allowed it to be open to an "external" presence—a divine force or a natural cause or a transcendent norm—that was the *real* agent of the self. This could be expressed in rebellion against an evil monarch (divinity in its goodness urges humans to rebel), or in violation of the social rules of gendered silence (women speak out when possessed of the Spirit). But extreme passion is regarded as incoherence—as temporary loss of self to external destructive forces—in respectable religion and in institutionalized politics as well as generally in everyday life.

IV

I want now to think further about the tension between the private self and its public mask in the context of political uncertainty. Masks are not simply devices for announcing one's persona to the world: they also hide secrets and offer themselves as misleading signs to be read by one's opponents. But the interpretation of signs is not entirely controllable by the mask's wearer: the reader may have his own agenda. So what might Mauss's notion of the mask tell us about relationships between the modern state and its free and equal citizens? It is often remarked that liberals mistrust power and that this is the source of liberal distrust of democracy. The state has reasons for mistrusting citizens—for suspecting that the law may be dangerously violated or that the power of the people may lead to undesirable consequences. But power is not merely an instrument for defending citizens; it is ultimately the state's very reason for existing.

Treason as a crime against the modern state is, so we might suppose, entirely a pragmatic, secular affair. And although personal betrayal is an ancient theme, the attachment of treason to the nation-state is relatively new. After all, if the state is seriously endangered, the collective life it enables may also be undermined.

But that practical concern doesn't fully explain the powerful emotions expressed in the discourse of political leaders and ordinary citizens confronted by treason. The state crime of treason is not defined in terms of damage inflicted by the traitor to national interests; what matters above all is giving "aid and comfort to the enemy." The U.S. Espionage Act of 1917, for example, does not require proof of "material harm" when deciding guilt. Pointing to treason tends to provoke anxiety and revulsion, a feeling that something deserving reverence has been besmirched, and a desire to inflict severe punishment on the traitor who has deceived not only the state but the nation, which the state symbolizes. As long ago as the eighteenth century, Jean-Jacques Rousseau articulated ideologically the ruthless necessity of exercising state power in the form of "the Terror" during the French Revolution: "every malefactor, by attacking social rights, becomes on forfeit a rebel and a traitor to his country; by violating its laws he ceases to be a member of it; he even makes war upon it. In such a case the preservation of the State is inconsistent with his own, and one or the other must perish; in putting the guilty to death, we slay not so much the citizen as the enemy."[26] In other words, the use of terror by the state against citizens who are hidden or discovered enemies is not merely justified because it is necessary for the state's survival; it is morally required because it addresses the security of the lives and properties of its citizens.[27] It is not that treason consists in breaking the law; violating the country's law is what traitors do.

These reactions suggest that treason is felt to resemble what the secular imagination thinks of as the religious emotion evoked by blasphemy, a supposed transgression against the deity himself. At work here is not simply the question of whether someone has seriously violated the law or not but of finding the traitor, a deeply immoral and duplicitous person. This ought to strike one as strange, if only because morality in modern society is supposed to be based on personal conscience, and the secular state is required to be impersonal and neutral. The modern state has no conscience, and even if its officials have, they are required to carry out their duties impersonally.

The discourse of President Woodrow Wilson, who introduced the Espionage Act of 1917, is puzzling if we insist on seeing the modern state as entirely unemotional and amoral. But it is the idea of the people's government and not its state that is at work here. In his December 1915 State of the Union address, Wilson urges Congress to pass it and stresses that while he has "no thought of any immediate or particular danger arising out of our relations with other nations," he nevertheless finds that "the gravest threats against our national peace and safety have been uttered within our own borders."[28] He is ashamed, he says, to admit that there were naturalized citizens of the United States "who have poured the poison of disloyalty into the very arteries of our national life; who have sought to bring the authority and good name of our Government into contempt, . . . and to debase our politics to the uses of foreign intrigue." These disloyal citizens—mostly immigrants—disturbed Wilson because they had, as he puts it, "brought deep disgrace upon us." He doesn't mention "Jews" and "Italians" but because socialists and anarchists were strongly represented in these two minorities, and because they were largely very recent immigrants, they were targets by implication. So in urging Congress to deal with this threat as quickly as possible, he assures it that he is urging them to do nothing less than "save the honor and self-respect of the nation." He goes on to say that although these treasonous persons are not many, "such creatures of passion, disloyalty, and anarchy must be crushed out" because "they are infinitely malignant." They had, apparently, formed plots to destroy property, conspired against "the neutrality of the Government," and tried to extract government secrets in order to serve "interests alien to our own." Wilson returns to the question of numbers: "I wish that it could be said that only a few men, misled by mistaken sentiments of allegiance to the governments under which they were born, had been guilty of disturbing the self-possession and misrepresenting the temper and principles of the country. . . . But it cannot." These people have no regard "for the peace and dignity of the United States." Wilson is reminding his audience of the risk that immigrants constitute, their attachment to a past that should be shed once they have entered a new state/status (i.e., once they have become naturalized citizens). Of course, he was aware that law itself could not reach the "corruptions of the mind and heart" of these traitors but an appropriate act would respond to the "humiliation and scorn which every self-possessed and thoughtfully patriotic American must feel when he thinks of them and of the discredit they are daily bringing upon us." Although what is known as the Red Scare in America really got going *after* the Espionage Act of 1917 was passed—indeed even after World War I had ended—Wilson's address anticipated the embittered atmosphere, to which he himself contributed, and which destroyed the early labor movement in America. Wilson's language is remarkable: sometimes downplaying the damage done by treacherous immigrants, sometimes exaggerating it, but above all invoking "the honor" of the nation's collective personality and adverting to "the poison of disloyalty [poured] into the very arteries of [America's] national life" by the presence within the country's borders of immigrant-conspirators. What is striking about this discourse is the strong moralism generated by—and generating—suspicion. (Writing about the ideological features of all political ideologies, including nationalism, Arendt noted that "the concept of enmity is replaced by that of conspiracy, and this produces a mentality in which reality—real enmity or real friendship—is no longer experienced and understood in its own terms but is automatically assumed to signify something else."[29]) Those who think that religious language can be a means of inspiring or criticizing the modern state's behavior underestimate the degree to which there is already a moral language available to the state to justify its representation of the nation. Wilson's suspicion of hidden words and motives exemplifies the desire for certainty in the task of ensuring security in an increasingly uncertain world.[30]

Betrayal once had religious meaning, and arguably it is this, translated into modern secular society, that gives it a passionate moral charge. (Passion—"enthusiasm"—we may recall, is what the Enlightenment thinkers attributed to "religion" as opposed to "reason.") Perhaps the most famous story of treason is Judas's betrayal of Jesus, of God incarnate Himself—an act essential to the founding of a great new religion based on the drama of redemption.[31] In the middle of the seventeenth century a Scottish lawyer classified blasphemy, witchcraft, and heresy together as instances of "Treason against God."[32] If blasphemy was thought of as treason against God, how different is treason against the sovereign when God is absent? Although God cannot betray his creatures, is it possible for the state to betray its citizens? If the state is the projection of the individual citizen (Manent: "I command myself through the intermediary of the government. In the end, I obey only myself"[33]), the secrets of citizens should not be secrets from the elected government that is empowered by the people to act through the state. Of course, constitutions (in states that have them) guarantee rights of privacy. But then the state is also tasked with protecting citizens not only from external enemies but also from the destructive instincts of other citizens—as Hobbes argued. And if its first and overriding duty is to maintain its integrity regardless of the damage that might do, the state may need to violate the privacy that hides the (possibly dangerous) thoughts, actions, and discourse of some of its citizens. Whether that violation is a betrayal is a difficult question.

Individual identification with the state also leads to the emergence of voluntary informers.[34] The state itself employs systems of spies (*agents provocateurs*) whose business is to build up trust in appropriate quarters in order to extract secrets and betray the trust of those from whom the secrets are obtained. It is always possible to make a case for preemptive action: persons whose statistical profile indicates that they incline toward treason and violence should be followed and apprehended under controlled circumstances before it is too late; their true motives can then be extracted. The line between identifying potential political treason and creating it by means of entrapment is not always easy to draw. This reflects an ambiguity in the modern state in which risks are at once identified and constructed.

Since the Second World War, the United States has been not merely a modern secular state; it is a superpower that protects its own position by finding actual and potential enemies not only within but also beyond its borders. This means being proactive against various forms of hostility—treason and terrorists at home, militant movements abroad. The state needs not only to confront foreign states militarily but also to engage in proxy wars and counterinsurgency and to infiltrate foreign societies. A passage from a School of the Americas manual titled *Handling of Sources* recommends: "The CI [counterintelligence] agent should consider all organizations as possible guerrilla sympathizers. . . . By infiltrating informants in the diverse youth, workers, political, business, social and charitable organizations, we can identify the organizations that include guerrillas among their members."[35] Surveillance takes place by infiltration, and its purpose is to look for signs of actual or potential betrayal—signs of possibility that need to be translated into *certainty* so that appropriate action can be taken. Although historically this has meant the presence of a secret informer in a targeted group, there are now more sophisticated ways of surveillance at a distance, using information technology, that are less easy for the targeted group to discover. The genealogy of surveillance as an expression of political suspicion, at whose center is the *sign*, remains to be written.

In his monograph *Paranoid Modernism*, David Trotter recounts an important part of the story. In it he describes the complex co-emergence of several elements of modern culture at the turn of the nineteenth century. He recounts how paranoia came to be identified and defined as a pathological form of suspicion in the development of modern psychiatry and psychoanalysis, which he relates to a profound and far-reaching change in nineteenth-century British society. What is particularly relevant in this for Trotter's history is the fact that the members of a growing middle class (what Gouldner identified as the educated middle class) find their importance no longer clearly defined: their status is acquired neither by property (land or capital) nor by labor but by competitive merit. This is the era in which imaginative literature increasingly deals with and reflects paranoia, both personal and political, and in which, incidentally, spy stories flourish.

The paranoiac, Trotter points out, rejects contingency and finds meaning in accidental events by which he confirms his belief that no one can be trusted: a smiling face, a friendly gesture, is a mask for hostile intent. The paranoiac is both a moralist and a translator. For him the mask is not simply a physical device that happens to conceal the real face; it is a *sign* that must be properly interpreted—and a proper reading and translation of the sign when based on a system gives it its real meaning. Systems therefore need to be constructed by rejecting contingency: "Paranoia cannot abide mess," Trotter writes.[36]

The process of becoming-paranoid has been consistently and inventively imagined by English writers since at least the time of the French Revolution: the formal and irreversible institution in France, in theory if not in practice, of bourgeois democracy. No doubt paranoia existed before the Revolution. But the creation of a stable ecological niche for the disease does seem to date from that period. . . . The demise of the *ancien régime* could be conceived, and not just by mad people, as the demise of a system which underwrote the attribution of social identity. Gods and emperors radiate well-being because they know who they are; without ever becoming one of them, we absorb the radiance, which we have after all created through our variously attentive acts of worship. But who or what was Robespierre? And how could he ever be sure that the world saw him as he saw himself?[37]

Trotter answers by pointing to the opportunities afforded the professional classes, including professional politicians, to demonstrate through competition superior expertise in an increasingly secularized society. One's claim to merit when faced with the claims of others generates an unease from which it is all too easy to slip into paranoia. Paranoia about being betrayed (the omnipresence of treason) is an obsession of the autonomous individual as well as the sovereign nation.[38]

When the meaning of actions in ordinary life is seen as uncertain, it may signal danger. Here is an interesting example from Michael Wood's discussion of a very early Hitchcock movie called *The Lodger*. Its ending, writes Wood, shows

that innocence and guilt can be represented by exactly the same story and the same signs. The point is not that there is no difference between them but that there is no difference between their representations. . . . *The Lodger* is based on a play, which in turn was based on a rather good novel, also called *The Lodger*, by Marie Belloc Lowndes. There the lodger is guilty, a man with a religious mania he takes out on women. But the mood of the novel is in many ways similar to that of Hitchcock's film. If in the film we worry about what the signs of guilt can mean if they don't mean guilt, in the novel the chief characters, the husband and wife who house the lodger, worry about what to do with their suspicions of their tenant's activities. They can't go to the police, because they're afraid of getting tangled up with the law, which they are sure can come to no good; and at the end of the novel they are grimly awaiting (but not really expecting) some kind of release—maybe someone will catch the killer, or he will move somewhere else. What's more, they don't just suspect their tenant, they know he's guilty and have proof that satisfies them even if it might not satisfy the police. They have to call their knowledge suspicion because they're afraid of it, and at one point the husband has these truly Hitchcockian thoughts: "The most awful thing about it all was that he wasn't sure.... If only he really knew! If only he could feel quite sure! And then he would tell himself that he had very little to go upon; only suspicion—suspicion, and a secret, horrible certainty that his suspicion was justified." Hitchcock's trick is to unjustify the ordinarily justifiable suspicion, and underline the horror of the wrong certainty. Well, of the right one too.[39]

In short, Wood reminds us that looking for the meaning of an action, event, or situation—translating doubt into certainty, as in a religious experience—presupposes that it is essentially a sign. Instead of simply grasping everyday language competently, "knowing how to go on," our desire for certainty in perceived uncertainty pushes us to interpret signs definitively, to express the rule according to which their meaning must be sought—and in that very process our suspicions may be reinforced. In such a situation, interpretation feeds on uncertainty, and uncertainty on interpretation. Suspicion avoids coming to a conclusion. For ordinary life to go on, the mastery of ordinary language and ordinary activity must take the place of interpretation. Is every action, every event, every thing a sign? A paranoiac would say yes. Paranoia, by definition, is the making of all actions, all events, all things into interpretable signs. One may put it this way: Everything that calls for an interpretation presents itself first as an ambiguous sign. But calculation, so it is claimed, is a sure way of avoiding ambiguity and uncertainty.

The delusions of the paranoiac, says Trotter, usually center on his conviction that he is important precisely because he faces enmity: he is envied by many because he is important, and his importance is confirmed by the fact that he is threatened by many.[40] Strictly speaking, this is not in itself the structure of a pathological state (as, for example, in Stalinist Russia[41]) but it does indicate a condition that promotes or reinforces paranoia among those who exercise its power. Nationalism thrives on grievances and suspicion of outsiders—especially outsiders concealed "within." But although the search for traitors is typically intended to identify individuals, the state's ideology of unconditional loyalty to the nation is a logical prerequisite. Of course, individuals do have a sense of solidarity toward groups, but these groups are not as homogeneous, clear-cut, and stable as is the state's definition of "the nation" from whose members loyalty is unconditionally demanded.

Treason is not, of course, the only kind of criminality of concern to the modern state. Criminal law deals with a wide range of offenses, and law enforcement has become a major issue in the contemporary politics of liberal democracies. In this context, the government's concern is no longer simply to respond to instances of law breaking when they happen but to anticipate them by employing actuarial techniques—that is, by compiling demographic tables on the basis of which criminality and delinquency can be predicted with varying degrees of probability in particular categories of the population and in particular neighborhoods. This has also become the technique par excellence for identifying the probable incidence of treason and terrorism through police profiling and secretly penetrating particular communities—especially since September 11, 2001—which of course contributes to undermining trust between community members.

We are confronted here, therefore, not only with the pathologies of doubt but also with conceptualizing uncertainty in mathematical terms and with ways of overcoming it (or at least controlling it) by means of a language of calculation.

V

So profiling is a way the state anticipates potential traitors, terrorists, and criminals. Profiling is at once a political and a commercial technique as well as a process of translation through computation.

In his study of the increasing use of actuarial tools in law enforcement in the United States, Bernard Harcourt writes:

> Most of us view this trend with hope, rather than alarm. With the single and notable, but limited exception of racial profiling against African Americans and Hispanics on the highways, most scholars, criminal justice practitioners, and public citizens embrace the turn to actuarial methods as a more efficient, rational, and wealth-maximizing tool to allocate scarce law enforcement resources. When we want to identify violent sexual predators, drug traffickers, tax cheats, or dangerous recidivists, we increasingly put our faith in actuarial instruments. The simple fact is, the police can detect more crime with the same resources if they investigate suspects who are more likely to offend, and courts can reduce crime more effectively if they imprison for longer periods convicted criminals who are more likely to return to crime. Most of us believe that the use of reliable actuarial methods in criminal law represents progress. No one, naturally, is in favor of spurious stereotypes and erroneous predictions. But to most of us, it simply makes common sense to decide whom to search based on reliable predictions of criminal behavior, or whom to incarcerate based on dependable estimates of future reoffending. It has become

second nature to think about just punishment through the lens of actuarial prediction [42]

Harcourt observes that this view is fundamentally mistaken because if the purpose of law enforcement is to reduce the level of crime in society, then predictability on the basis of profiling will actually increase the number of those identified as criminals. However, if the purpose is to anticipate crime, then an increase in the numbers of arrest and indictment (on the basis of the behavioral response to policing of those profiled) proves the actuarial method a success. This applies to a range of crimes, from drug trafficking and robbery to terrorism and treason, in which profiling is a step in the unmasking of criminals. Paradoxically, to be proactive, to anticipate the future, is in a significant measure to *make* it part of the present. The language of numbers as an instrument of modern rule is intimately connected to the construction of social categories, quantification to representation according to what Ian Hacking has called "the looping effect."[43]

Everyone is familiar with the fact that the collection of statistical data is an important means for the state to profile individuals who might break the law—whether as petty criminals or as terrorists or as political protesters—and thus to disable those who constitute a challenge to its power and authority. But profiling is simply one way of identifying lawbreakers and troublemakers by targeting suspicious groups to which such individuals belong. Today governments and commercial corporations share statistical techniques that begin not with a priori categories (such as ethnicity or religious affiliation or neighborhood) but with the personal characteristics (behavior, beliefs, interaction patterns, tastes, etc.) of vast numbers of individuals in order to identify clusters by which groups of individuals might be identified and thus targeted—not only as potential criminals but also, and perhaps more importantly, as consumers or voters. The clusters in this case are the products of computational methods, they are not preexisting cultural groups. Because the groups constructed mathematically (by information-collecting agencies: private businesses and government departments independently or in collaboration with one another) are unknown to the individuals who are classified as belonging to them, they are unable to resist manipulative power as a solidary group precisely because they do not know the other members of the group. In this sense the relative strength of self-constituting groups (whether inherited or not) in confronting the increasing power of the state is greatly diminished.[44]

VI

Perhaps one should be thinking not only about treason and other forms of criminality that justify suspicion and proactive moves by the nation-state but also about how "national solidarity" itself is protected and created. This would help us to see better similarities between the modern state's surveillance and the posture of the paranoiac, when, in circumstances of perceived danger, the minds of citizens are confronted as illegible. There is, however, a crucial difference between the two: unlike the individual paranoiac, the modern state doesn't simply look for what it sees as threats nesting in the gap between "public behavior" and "real intention" in order to protect itself. It seeks to remake citizens in its image.

In his book titled *The New Social Question*, Pierre Rosanvallon notes that by the eighteenth century "there were three available models for conceiving of the social bond: the contract (resulting from a conscious political decision), the market (operating as an invisible hand linking men economically), and insurance (acting as an invisible hand of solidarity)."[45] All three use numbers: the choice by national elections of those who will govern, the state of the market economy that sustains and is guarded by the liberal state, and caring for the life needs of its citizens. In all three situations, the language of numbers seeks to translate contingency into degrees of probability so that even where uncertainty cannot be totally eliminated it can be quantified and thus manipulated by actuarial techniques.

Rosanvallon doesn't pursue the differences between these models of the modern state, in which the first is idealized (typically expressed in a written constitution); the second, crucial in new ways to finance capitalism (thus promoting social disparities and aggravating resentments); and the third includes the mutually incompatible values of collective responsibility as well as of self-interest (insurance as a response to human need, on the one hand, and insurance as a response to profit-making and government control on the other).

After the establishment of the United States (the first modern republic) the American political elite began to be troubled by the familiar theme of the decline and fall of republics. William Adams confronted his audience: "All history has chronicled the same story—those who would be free, baffled by their own success, and buried by their own triumphs—independence leading to wealth, wealth to luxury, luxury to impatience of control, and this, by rapid stages, to effeminacy, corruption, vassalage, and destruction."[46] Political contracts embodied in constitutions were not sufficient. "Our liberties may be secured in charters and constitutions," Adams pointed out, "but who or what shall guarantee us against the excesses of liberty but self-control in the individual man?"[47] The answer to that way of posing the problem for many among the elites in the late eighteenth and nineteenth centuries was the need to develop a national culture that would be reflected in the disciplined character of individual citizens.

Although the specter of republican decline was banished during the subsequent period of rapid industrialization and territorial expansion, it has returned in more recent decades to highlight an increasing disjunction between the ideals of the constitution and the unrestrainable ambitions of the political, military, and financial elites. The social divisions produced by the increasingly deregulated economy have been unprecedented in degree, but political instability—at least within national territory—has been contained by an entertainment culture and by organizations (some formally part of the state, some not) that are tasked with the maintenance of legal order. This combination of state and contracted enterprise (both being subject to the constitution) uses highly sophisticated technologies of surveillance and control as well as the language of statistics for formulating risk and thus seeks to penetrate the masks of potential disrupters. But secularization's greatest achievement lies in the future, in eliminating decisively the distance between the mask and its wearer.

European thinkers and politicians have come to regard the institutionalization of insurance as a solution to the major dilemma produced by a secularizing liberal society: it reconciles the principle of solidarity (the nation owes a debt to all who belong) with the principle of responsibility (each person alone owns her life). The language in which this reconciliation has been expressed is statistics, and what is remarkable about it is not merely its secularity (probability theory is a rational way of dealing with uncertainty without resort to divine powers) but its ability to reconstruct individual and collective freedom. The modern, territorial state is tasked not only with the life and death of its citizens against physical attack (defense) but also with securing their health and welfare (biopolitics).

Rosanvallon points out that economic and technological developments in the nineteenth and twentieth centuries have made this seeming reconciliation highly questionable by blurring the boundaries between social solidarity and individual responsibility, between equal rights and unequal choice. "As the social cost of individual attitudes appears more distinctly," he observes, "solidarity and freedom will part company."[48] His example: the smoker who insists on his freedom to smoke but will increasingly be seen as someone who doesn't have an equal right to health care provided, in some form or other, by the state. But the decline of national insurance is not necessarily, so Rosanvallon notes, a decline of national solidarity.

There are, however, questions vital to the problem of solidarity that he doesn't address: First, how the practice of insurance has evolved in the liberal state and shaped or misshaped solidarity; second, closely connected with the latter question, how the increasing investment of savings in financial markets, a process strongly encouraged by the liberal state has become "democratized";[49] third, how immigrants from ex-colonial countries (and more recently, refugees from the South generally) have challenged it. All these questions concern how far and in what form mutual responsibility and uncertainty of the intentions of others can extend within and beyond the secular nation-state. And all of them deploy the language of numbers.

In what follows, I focus on a very small part of the fascinating history of insurance.

VII

In the early encounter with life insurance, many believers disapproved of it on the grounds that it was an attempt to anticipate and so interfere with God's will. Precisely for that reason, however, others argued that insurance and probability theory demonstrated the superiority of secular knowledge over religious belief.[50]

The approach to insurance from the point of view of an ethically informed law is not unusual, of course. In *Classical Probability in the Enlightenment*, Lorraine Daston argues that "seventeenth-century legal practices and theories shaped the first expression of mathematical probability and stamped the classical theory with two of its most distinctive and enduring features: the 'epistemic' interpretation of probabilities as degrees of certainty; and the primacy of the concept of expectation."[51]

So there is more to the history of insurance (whether undertaken by for-profit companies, by the state, or by local groups) than yet another triumph of rational thinking, more than simply the development of mathematical techniques to be used in situations of uncertainty or ignorance, and neither is modern insurance merely an expression of the growth of solidarity. It represents a radical shift in the scope and direction of mutual responsibility and aid—and therefore of the kind of society it encourages. In this shift, statistics were accumulated, parsed, and put into motion by the centralized nation-state and its corporate allies—including, most importantly, the stock exchange.

Thus, in nineteenth-century Britain, as in other parts of the early capitalist (or, indeed, pre-capitalist) world, workers organized themselves to take care of one another's personal and family needs on the basis of "friendship, brotherly-love, and charity" in what were therefore known as friendly societies. "A study of the practices of friendly societies in this period," writes Peter Gosden, a British historian of mutual aid societies, "throws some light on the way in which the 'industrious classes' sought to let a little entertainment and colour enter their drab lives. In the early years the convivial activity of the societies was of the utmost importance, and . . . as an essential part of the life of any self-respecting society. The ritual of initiation, the good fellowship of the lodge room and the celebrations of the annual 'club day' meant much to members."[52] These rituals expressed feelings of friendship and affirmed local solidarity, in which members shared a form of life. It was not "egalitarianism" that the societies aspired to achieve or a substitute for what their lives "really" lacked (a little entertainment and color); it was practical concern for the misfortunes of life that befall all human beings who live together. But against their will, a new language was being introduced.

According to some estimates, there were several thousand such societies that existed in the country by the end of the eighteenth century.[53] Unlike later arrangements, however, friendly societies covered only sickness, incapacity, and funeral expenses; income after retirement was not provided. In fact, given the fluidity of labor and laboring at the time, the category "retirement" didn't crystallize until much later, after the decline of the friendly societies and the emergence of old-age pensions provided by the state and (later) by for-profit insurance companies. This was the period when the modern state and modern society reciprocally formed each other, a period that witnessed the development of class conflicts and class strategizing, when state power emerged increasingly as the answer to problems of social solidarity and security.[54]

As the state grew in its scope and ambition, the legality of friendly societies was subjected to increasing suspicion among the governing elite and the eventual imposition of computational language.[55] The reason for this suspicion was in part due to the fact that they offered not only social support to members of the working class but also political experience at a time when conventional state institutions (parliament, local government, etc.) excluded any direct working-class presence.[56] This historical shift can be seen as a further awareness of masks—and therefore of the need to dissemble and to read signs of disloyalty—from courtiers to ordinary subjects. In retrospect, therefore, friendly societies came to be seen in two contradictory ways: on the one hand as part of the history of worker solidarity that was eventually able to join in putting pressure on the ruling elite to create a welfare state, and on the other hand as an example, of private initiative that was allegedly both possible and desired by the working class before it was co-opted into dependence on the state (libertarians prefer dependence on those who dominate the market—which they call "enterprise").[57] In both cases, the law's ascendency in the definition and regulation of insurance (and of defining, retrospectively, violation of the law) was made possible by statistics, a language indispensable to private corporations as well as to the modern state.

Hostility from the governing elite toward friendly societies remained strong.[58] For the elite that governed the state, the existence of friendly societies met with skepticism about the claim that they would help to lower the financial cost of supporting the poor and, more important, generated anxiety about possible working-class treason. In the eyes of the nation's ruling class, the intentions of working-class societies expressing the interests of local communities were always opaque; the abstract language of statistics eventually offered itself as the best way of reformulating uncertainty and of anticipating the risk of insubordination and even, possibly, treason.

Although parliament monitored the friendly societies in the first three quarters of the nineteenth century, and they were therefore not entirely independent of the state even then, it was not until the Societies Act of 1875 that they were required to register with the Registrar of Friendly Societies, particularly if they wanted to own property and to undertake legal proceedings. Registration required them to be subjected to unprecedented regulation by the registrar requiring proper auditing, rates of incoming and outgoing monies in relation to the requirements of solvency, and, in general, what was described as the adoption of "sound rules" for running insurance enterprises. In time, the state's imposition of "sound scientific principles" (i.e., life insurance tables, balanced budgets, and so forth) on these mutual aid societies served not only to change their financial basis but also eventually to undermine the value of human need and unconditional support they expressed.[59] The turn to risk management, produced by state demand and the use of probability theory (based on the collection of information about the ages and other personal circumstances of members, and on rules about eligibility, monthly contributions, and final benefits), amounted in effect to a shift away from the values the friendly societies had earlier sought and toward a profoundly different pattern of interpersonal relations directed or regulated by the state. The friendly society did not seek to make a profit by calculating the probabilities of illness and death of the members collectively, did not need actuarial tables and calculations to ensure profit at the end of the day, as modern insurance firms do.

So the increasing use of statistics for insurance as well as for innumerable other political purposes expresses the increasing need of the developing state to overcome uncertainties in trying to read and deal with the hidden intentions of large numbers of subjects.[60]

VIII

It is interesting that attitudes to risk are now changing as a result not only of the increasing privatization of insurance as a measure of increasing efficiency but also of the reconceptualization of risk itself in positive terms: the idea is widely promoted that too much protection is bad for people's material and psychological development, for the national economy as well as for individual character. Thus, from the older view that risk is something to be avoided or managed, it is now sought in a considerable range of individual behavior, especially in the context of the stock market, where it has become the principal source of wealth generation (and cause of wealth loss) through the process known as "securitization." Although in many matters (the public consumption of food and pharmaceuticals, the results of military operations, etc.[61]) there is a contradictory demand for minimizing or avoiding foreseeable harm altogether, the encouragement of a flexible individualism claimed to be appropriate for the challenges of new capitalism is increasingly—and triumphantly—described as "competing on the edge" and as "embracing risk."[62] This culture fits well with Goffman's vision of a society of strategizing individuals who are masked in the public domain, and of efficiency as the ultimate norm of success. The increase of this kind of competitive individualism obviously fragments the experience of one's membership in a collectivity that has become abstract, making the sense of mutual trust and responsibility among individuals more difficult to achieve. In place of trust there is an increase of suspicion. (Thus, in March 2017 I received a notification from my bank warning me to be alert and suspicious of all communications: "Don't assume that anyone who sends a text or calls you is who they say they are.") In a society where masks confront one another, where the management of risk is the primary challenge and primary opportunity, and where time is broken time, discursive tradition becomes increasingly difficult to maintain.[63]

The dismantling of the welfare state by neoliberal policies did not, of course, mean the dismantling of the state. On the contrary, neoliberalism, in contrast to classical economic theory, depends on a strong state that ensures a market-based society and economy by fiscal austerity, privatization, deregulation, unrestricted free trade, and the strategic restriction of civil rights where these conflict with business interests. With their close connections to industrial and financial corporations, mediated by (private) banks and the (state) military, Western neoliberal states have also become global war states, often working through proxies against possible global threats, especially the threat to energy resources. One well-known result of using state violence and terror has been to destabilize entire regions in the Middle East and Africa and consequently to generate and reinforce nonstate terrorism—and so to ramp up more fear and anxiety among ordinary citizens, more calls for increased state security and what some are calling the militarization of Western liberal democracies.[64] There seems to be too much investment, financial and ideological, for this to be changed: particular interests triumph over collective concerns.

War, incidentally, is not without important domestic consequences. Over the last two centuries, total war has not simply been the violent warding off by the state of external threat and the creation of a sentiment of national solidarity—guided crucially by the nation-state. It has provided an opportunity for constructing a secular citizenry through legal and administrative technologies.[65] Crucial to those techniques, again, is mathematical language whose use extends far beyond the project of insurance within the modern state, a language indispensable not only for policies relating to the economy, crime, health, education, and so on, but also for scientific and technological research.

As this use has grown, so have complaints about the misleading character of particular statistics. However, probability theory is not only an indispensable language for modern state policies, it is also admirably constructed for public argument. (The very first introductory book on statistics that I bought and read, in 1958, was entitled *How to Lie with Statistics*, which taught the elementary grammar of that language.) But it should be stressed that beyond the fact that statistics can be argued over by representing and misrepresenting social reality, the language of mathematics *remakes* it.[66] In the *Theses on Feuerbach*, Marx famously wrote: "The philosophers have only *interpreted* the world, in various ways. The point, however, is to *change* it." That slogan works most efficiently when the secular language of mathematics translates reality into numbers by which it can then regulate and reinvent the world.

Statistical data and mathematical techniques generally were historically important not only for purposes of modern government but also, and reciprocally, for the development of secular society. It is not simply that the modern state depends crucially on mathematics: the capitalist economy does too, because both the state and the economy are inextricably interconnected—even in highly deregulated economies.[67]

Thus, Martijn Konings sums up the fundamental shift in the character of late capitalism as follows:

> Contemporary capitalism should be understood not as a process whereby speculative financial forms become disconnected from fundamental values but in terms of the interacting imperatives of speculation and austerity. The financial measure of neoliberal life owes its resilience to the affective charge generated by the tension between the inescapable need to engage contingency and the promise that the faithful engagement of risk may itself become a source of economic and spiritual certainties.[68]

An obvious result of these changes is that the possibilities of mutual responsibility and the social solidarity based on it are increasingly shifted into—and diminished in—a world of masked individuals.

IX

I now conclude with another aspect of the problem of national solidarity in a secular world and the language that problem deploys. I propose that the liberal democratic state is secular because and to the extent that it depends crucially on the language of numbers: it is calculation that finally determines to whom the state belongs.

In chapter 1 I wrote: "Whether the modern state—whose overriding commitment is to maintain itself and its power whatever it takes—is capable of responding to moral suasion, and, if so, then in what language, is a question Habermas doesn't address." A friend who read the sentence in the original draft suggested that it is precisely by invoking "the nation" (equal bodies within an inclusive solidary body) that a moral demand for inclusivity can be made. This is an important point, and it is certainly how appeals to the state are often made. I am troubled, however, for two main reasons: first, by the ease with which exclusivist definitions of "the nation" can be used to buttress state authority ("the *real* nation is 'Aryan,' or 'Anglo-Saxon,' or 'Jew,' or 'Muslim,' or 'Hindu,' etc."); and second, because the modern state itself requires ideological exclusion from the imagined "national culture."[69] And "national culture" is inevitably tied to the numerical majority. The latter reason is particularly concerning because the state has tasks (defending the lives and property of its citizens) that can be used to legitimate its discriminatory power: the realization and integrity of the nation-state must be maintained regardless of moral and material damage to others if this is unavoidable.

Liberals tend to regard the construction of a modern state, whose identity depends on the numerical majority, as the moral right of "a people" (viz., "a nation"). As an example of such an argument I turn to an article, by the British journalist Jonathan Freedland, that deals with the establishment of Israel.[70] This state is interesting for several reasons, including the fact that it was made possible by the support of the Great European Powers for motives both religious and secular. Apart from being based on considerations of imperial strategy, it was the secular answer to Christianity's "Jewish Problem"—at first theological and then racial—a form of European anti-Semitism accepted as "natural" by both Zionist Christians and Zionist Jews. Speaking of the early Zionists, virtually all of whom were atheists, the Israeli historian of ideas Amnon Raz-Krakotzkin writes: "One can summarize secular Zionism with the phrase: God does not exist but he promised the land to us."[71]

Freedland's symptomatic article translates a powerful ideological movement aiming to nationalize and overwhelm an already inhabited territory and to engineer a demographic configuration appropriate to a modern nation-state whose justification can be achieved by translating a settler-colonial conquest into a human image: a chance encounter between two individuals both struggling against the deadly force of nature, formally equal but mutually exclusive. "Besides the legal right bestowed by the UN's 1947 resolution to partition Palestine into two states, one Jewish and one Arab," Freedland writes,

> Israel had a moral right—the right of the drowning man. Such a man is entitled to grab hold of a piece of driftwood even if another man is already holding it. The drowning man can even make the other man share it, by force, if necessary. His moral right ends, however, the moment he pushes the other man into the sea. The Jewish people, scythed by the Holocaust and after centuries of persecution, were gasping for breath in 1948; their need for a home was as great as that of any people in history. They had the right to act, even though the cost for another people, the Palestinians, was immense.[72]

By translating a nation-making project into an individual's instinct to survive, Freedland equates the *moral* right of a man to save his life with the *political* right to self-determination of a settler-colonial state to come into existence as a state. Land on which inhabitants have lived for centuries is translated into driftwood that no one owns, and to some unknown catastrophe that brings two survivors together in the same wreckage. Freedland invokes the UN's 1947 resolution that assigned part of a British colonial territory (Mandate Palestine) to "a future Jewish state" but does not mention that the land assigned in that resolution to "a future Palestinian state" was annexed, after the expulsion of its Palestinian inhabitants, by the newly declared state of Israel—because without that ethnic cleansing, the Jewish state would not have been demographically or territorially viable.[73] There is no question of sharing here but of "this is mine, therefore it is not yours."

The image of two men threatened equally by accidental destruction accommodates the UN's 1948 Resolution no.194 that subsequently affirmed the right of Palestinian refugees to return to their homes in Israel (a resolution ignored by Israel since 1948).[74] Although many Israeli and non-Israeli Jews have spoken eloquently as individuals of the rights of Palestinian refugees driven from their homes, this matter cannot be a moral concern for the *state* of Israel; that state can recognize the rights only of incoming Jewish immigrants because it is a Jewish state. And it cannot undertake policies that might undermine its own demographic character.

This is also why the occupation and control of the West Bank and Gaza as separate entities can be maintained with the insistence that Israel is a liberal democratic state. "Modern imperialism," Carl Schmitt long ago pointed out,

has created countless new governmental forms, conforming to economic and technical developments, which extend themselves to the same degree that democracy develops within the motherland. Colonies, protectorates, mandates, intervention treaties, and similar forms of dependence make it possible today for a democracy to govern a heterogeneous population without making them citizens, making them dependent on a democratic state, and at the same time held apart from this state. That is the political and constitutional meaning of the nice formula "the colonies are foreign in public law, but domestic in international law."[75]

The influential political philosopher Michael Walzer has recently observed that the value of the state lies *only* in the protection it affords to the community or communities it contains. The state is the critically necessary agent of defense: against military attack, against natural disaster, against famine and disease, against poverty and the traumas of old age. All this is very important, and so a certain kind of patriotism—loyalty to the state as our common defense and participation in its politics—is legitimate and right.[76]

The proposition that the state is preeminently an agent of defense of "a community or communities" presupposes the existence of a clearly definable collectivity for which the defensive functions are carried out. But as defender and sustainer, the modern state is in fact a territorial power, at once sovereign and symbol of what it regards as a solidary community: "loyalty" in this context evokes the cognate sense of "obedience," an attitude rejected by the modern, secular value of "self-determination." Walzer goes on: "But it is the internal life of the communities that gives us, so to speak, a reason to live and a 'way of life' that we share with others—a language, a culture, a calendar, the rituals that mark the life cycle, the books with which we are most closely engaged, the vistas that we recognize."[77] But if the internal life of *one* community is not to be given preference by the state over the others, it is because the state is already an independent, secular power. However, what if the defense of "the internal life" of the majority community requires the maintenance of its majority? There are two points that need close attention here in considering state–community relations: (1) In representing "the community" as a unified body whose members are said to share a way of life, the state presents a public face of a homogeneous body to other states, a face that differs, especially in large modern states, from the domestic situation. (2) The state's claim to be defending the unity of the community is what legitimates its use of violence, secrecy, and coercion within national and nationally dependent territory; its obligation to defend a shared way of life is not quite how the state sees the community. The state doesn't merely represent and defend the community; it tries to make what is in effect a web of communal life into a nation, a unity in which a particular character is sought and maintained. It emphasizes what is to be remembered and what forgotten.

In his well-known essay "What Is a Nation?" Ernest Renan observes: "Forgetting, and I might even say historical error, is an essential factor in the creation of a nation, and this is why the progress of historical studies is often a danger to the principle of nationality. Historical investigation, in fact, brings to light the deeds of violence that took place at the origin of all political formations, even those whose consequence have been most fortunate."[78] What Renan does not say is that forgetting is directed not simply at the moment of origin but also at every moment when national character is affirmed. What is presupposed in the nation's existence, as he famously puts it, is not simply "a daily plebiscite" expressing, incidentally, the consent and desire to continue a common life through a numerical language, but a daily forgetting—a daily silence—of the continued cruelties, inflicted within and without the state, on which the nation's common life (its "self-determination") rests.[79]

Because internal conditions cannot be isolated from external dangers and attractions, the state demands loyalty from its citizens and subordination from its conquered subjects. Political loyalty is not simply a reasonable response from political subjects; it is an unconditional demand by centralized authority. What rarely gets systematic discussion (for obvious reasons) is what has been called "the deep state." It has been argued that, especially in the Middle East, the deep state consists not only of the police and intelligence services but also of the network that connects them to politicians, business interests, and organized crime, and that its members consider themselves to be the defenders of "the basic values" of the nation even when it requires them to violate the law and deny that they do so. But of course the deep state is simply one aspect of the modern state—liberal democracies included—whose viability depends on it as well as on international networks.[80]

In the modern world, state (sovereign territorial power) and community (shared way of life) are entangled in complicated ways. The conception of community that Walzer puts forward as the object of protection is virtually indistinguishable from the nineteenth-century understanding of the nation. The founding assumption in that understanding is that the nation is complete only when it is represented by a single sovereign state of its own—indeed, it is that function of representation and the powers claimed in its name that constitute the state. It is conceded, of course, that members of the same community may be citizens of several distinct territorial states. One result is that what appears as a moral right of the community (to be represented and defended by the state) may also appear as a political problem for the secular liberal state: nonnational populations within state territory may constitute a danger to the community's "shared culture and way of life," and since the state is committed to defending the community so defined (and to help make it a bounded community), it must exert its power to determine what must be shared and by whom. But the perception of discrimination and victimization by minority populations creates a sense of resentment that, in extreme situations, may be provoked into perpetrating acts of terror aimed at challenging the state's ability to defend the community—and that, in turn, may lead to the expansion of violence and terror used by the state, thus promoting a vicious cycle.

So to the question, "What gives the Zionist project its *moral* right—its right to self-determination?" the liberal answer is to stress that an independent state is *a right*. It is deserved and it is needed, and the fact that the Palestinians had nothing to do with the Holocaust in Europe, that they are nevertheless to be driven from their land, is irrelevant because the issue is the primordial right of Jews—like the right of every other people—to fulfill itself as a nation, regardless of the means.[81] The moral authority for establishing a "national home" is not contingent: it is not derived from an accidental history of persecution and of the need to end it by providing statehood. It derives from the nation's inherent right to be realized fully in an independent state—"even though the *cost* for another people," that is, even though the cruelty inflicted on them in establishing that state, was (thus Freedland) "immense." This moral right remains supreme even though the state cannot be the protector of all Jews living in various countries.[82] And what the state has done by establishing itself on the basis of a claim to an ancient connection to that land is to create something entirely new: an *Israeli nation* whose citizens live a form of life entirely different from that of Jews in Palestine two thousand years ago and much closer to the beliefs, aspirations, and forms of life characteristic of non-Jews in Europe and America. So the point to address is not that Israel defends Jews (as a state, it cannot defend Jews who are citizens of other states); it is to raise the following question: If the Israeli state claims to represent *only* all Jews (whether religious or nonreligious, whether residing in Israeli territory or not) how is its demand for loyalty from non-Jewish Israelis and non-Israeli Jews to be realized? Raz-Krakotzkin has argued that to answer this question requires coming to terms with the rich theological conception of Jewish exile, on the one hand, and the simplified modern notion of "new Jew" sought by the secular Zionist state, on the other.[83]

For liberalism, language is often a necessary political mask or a means of translation by which the truth can be disguised (when a good conscience is sought) from the speaker himself. Thus, when a liberal democracy begins to morph into a cruel, repressive state, it is often justified as a necessity or—tautologically—as a sign of immaturity.

So to speak of the "cost" to victims, as Freedland does in recounting his story, is less disturbing to liberal sensibilities than "cruelty" because it can be thought of as something that isn't the result of an arbitrary imposition but of market calculations. The American journalist George Packer recently wrote about the problem of "social cost" and especially about "how difficult the trade-off between liberty and security can be in a democratic society."[84] This kind of liberal agonizing expressed in a market metaphor appears more directly in the frequent appeal to "negotiation" in the conflict between the Israeli state and the Palestinian population—as though the enormous power disparity between the two sides can be expressed through the figure of a transaction between two merchants who wish to do business with each other. The authority of this kind of argument comes from the claim that we are dealing essentially with quantitative values, and even if striking a balance between gain and loss is sometimes difficult, numbers facilitate an objective conclusion.

Since the principle that defines the state as a state is the monopoly of legitimate violence, and since it possesses the technology to exercise violence and coercion against its own citizens (in the form of policing and domestic law) as well as on outsiders (in the form of war and the management of "alien" populations in sovereign or colonial territory), it needs to establish and maintain a convenient language that includes words and mathematical symbols for enabling its projects. Since the nation-state has claims to territory, and the territory has to be defined, defended, and when necessary extended, it will be necessary to undertake restrictive immigration (and/or ethnic cleansing) if "democracy" is to be plausibly claimed as the nation's political system. The convergence of the two forms of state violence (internal and external) is increasingly apparent in the contemporary nation-state.[85] This applies not only to Israel but also to the United States, Britain, Egypt, Pakistan, India, and all other real or aspiring liberal democracies.

So I return, finally, to Robert Skidelsky, whom I cited at the beginning of chapter 1: "Donald Trump's call to bar Muslims from the United States," he writes, provoked the following exchange with two young friends of mine: "If the choice was between Muslim immigration and preserving liberal moral values," I asked, "which would you choose?" They both denied the question's premise. The immigrants themselves, they suggested, might have reactionary moral codes, but their children, growing up in today's Britain, America, or Continental Europe, would be quite different.[86] But is that true? My question focused not on Islamist terrorism—the ostensible ground of Trump's outburst—but on the threat posed by large-scale Muslim immigration to the code of morals that my young friends, like most educated Europeans, now accept without question. Terrorism aside, wouldn't they worry if Islam came to have a growing influence on British law and politics?[87]

In expressing his moral panic, Skidelsky was telling his young listeners that the state requires a homogeneous national culture that had the moral and political right not to be challenged by public argument and political organization. Even if, unavoidably, there *is* a degree of religious or ethnic heterogeneity in society, there must be a clear and permanent demographic majority of those who know that the state belongs principally to them; minorities must be small enough to be easily controllable.[88] It is no accident that demography has been central to secularization in the history of Europe and to the formation of the exclusivist nation-state to which that history has given birth.[89]

Ideologically, the nation precedes the state because the state represents and protects the nation it represents; the state is the nation's offspring and guarantor.[90] In fact, it is more often the other way around. Thus, the use of violence to keep nonnationals out of national territory (or to remove them once they are inside) may become necessary for the sake of the nation's political health. There is therefore every reason to hold back a large influx of Muslim refugees—and even, in connection with that threat, to expel people of refugee origin.[91]

What I find most striking about Skidelsky's argument, however, is not that it treats a group identified by its religion invidiously in spite of his claim to being a liberal—it is, after all, the function of a secular democracy to identify religions or ideologies that are dangerous to "national values" without which the nation-state means little. What stands out is his confidence that we live in a world with a recognizable future.

X

But there are, finally, other developments of secular reason more troubling than the reality of Islamophobia and the creeping prospect of a repressive state based on fear. The future control of human populations may perhaps lie not in more effective surveillance but in the creation of new individuals through genetic engineering and artificial intelligence. When the thought, speech and behavior of "cyborg citizens" are completely separated from the embodied subject, when life itself is treated essentially as *information* that is capable of being removed from the "natural" body as its contingent carrier and translated through mathematical signs into a machine as its virtuality, there is then no longer a need to penetrate behind masks since there will be no "real" self to hide from power.[92] The crucial opposition here will no longer be between hidden intentions and public behavior but between the living body and the information that articulates it as a self. Once information is obtained from the "natural" body, there is no reason why it cannot be translated into an indefinite number of interconnected computers. When the particular materiality of the body is treated as accidental to its life—a "natural" life that is born, that learns, succeeds and fails, shares a form of life with others, feels pain, and dies; a life whose trace moves through generations of subsequent living beings—then the very sense of a discursive tradition is undermined.

The social science literature on this subject is already very considerable. Thus, for example, James Hughes's widely read *Citizen Cyborg* makes the following familiar claim: "In the twenty-first century the convergence of artificial intelligence, nanotechnology and genetic engineering will allow human beings to achieve things previously imagined only in science fiction. . . . We will merge with machines and machines will become more like humans."[93] Those who oppose this new trend Hughes contemptuously labels "bioLuddites," people "rejecting liberal democracy, science and modernity."[94] The only rational challenge of the scientific future, in his view, consists in ensuring that liberal democratic government provides all with an equitable distribution of access to the new developments. "The central propositions of this book," Hughes writes, "are that people are generally happier when they have more control over their own lives, and that technology and democracy are the two key ways by which we can exert more control over our lives."[95] So yet again one meets a confident secular assumption: that the sense of the "human" will be recognizable in that future, and so will continue to be the object of solicitude regardless of the increasing ability of the state to use violence and manipulation in its overriding commitment to maintain itself. To the extent that life becomes information (easily accessible, translatable, reproducible—and corruptible), it becomes a more far-reaching means of power that eliminates the distinction between a private self and a public presentation, or between an authentic identity and the mask it needs to wear in a suspicious world.[96]

And the distinction between "death" and "eternal life" disappears too.[97]

Epilogue

While I am not persuaded by the attempts of so many distinguished thinkers to translate Christianity into secularism, this is not because I think that secularism deserves to be defended from a non-Christian point of view.[1] My skepticism is based on the fact that we think of both "Christianity" and "secularity" too rigidly, describing them too confidently, on the basis of an a priori secular history and secular anthropology.[2] The very dispute over whether there is or is not an essential continuity between religion and the secular depends on constructed concepts of both. In this book I have been concerned mainly to problematize rigid uses of "secularity" and "religion"—which is not to say that I wish to condemn (or for that matter to advocate) the life their discourses regulate or invite one into. Current arguments about whether one should be for or against "modernity" seem to me unrewarding. If there is one general point this book has been making, it is that words like "modernity," "religion," "politics," "secularism" and their associated, shifting vocabularies are intertwined with modes of life. It is attention to the particular character of that intertwining, to what opponents claim or reject as the "proper" meaning of these terms (as their "essence") that should be our primary concern in trying to understand what people expect or demand from or dislike about "the secular" or "the religious"— and why they do so.[3] The terms "secularity" and "religion" belong to what Wittgenstein called language games, games within which consensus and dispute occur as part of ordinary life—games that are always capable of being changed, with or without agreement.

In thinking about secularization, I rely on no overarching theory, but I am attracted by Walter Benjamin's resort to theology as one way of exploring moral and political dimensions of thought, feeling, and action. One finds a concern with ethics in much of Benjamin's writing, especially in his "On the Concept of History"— one of the last things he wrote. I am thinking particularly of the famous section 9, which describes a Paul Klee painting of what Benjamin calls the angel of history thrown backward into the future by a storm ("that we call progress") blowing violently from Paradise (the promise of Paradise), and sees with horror the past as nothing more than accumulating debris. Benjamin spoke both the language of historical materialism and the language of theology, invoking both what he called profane time and messianic time— not as a matter of simple analogy but of mutual provocation, of helping to open up the possibility of a new language that is too often confused with a demand either for "spirituality" or for "sound reason." What worked so effectively in Benjamin's case might also work if we confronted anthropology with theology, not to encourage the former to build on the latter (still less, to translate "religion" opportunistically) but to draw on the latter to provoke the former— provocation being a way of overcoming the limitations of sterile habit. And why stop at theology? Why not also context-rich endeavors like poetry, cinema, and the arts generally?

Here is a thought that Benjamin's angel of history did not, I think, have: Our present—called by some Anthropocene rather than modernity—has seen our secular knowledge and our way of life generate unprecedented threats to all of global life: The

Ending of Time, originally the privilege of divinity, now reveals itself as a possible human fiat—hence, as theology in an ironic mode. The violence of industrialization and environmental exploitation over recent centuries has initiated global climate change and the collapse of the ecosystem and has accompanied astonishing advances in science and technology that, among other things, have made the violence of nuclear weapons real. In these connected developments, the systematic application of secular reason has opened up the prospect of ending all life on our planet. Is Benjamin's angel grieving also over our historical blindness?

In a reflection on the biblical myth of Adam and Eve and their loss of innocence, the philosopher Herbert Morris writes that one should not think that the sudden awareness of what is obvious to the eye (that they are both naked) is itself knowledge of good and evil. The former, says Morris, is the beginning of insight and, although moral knowledge begins with it, the full realization of that knowledge takes time.[4] Loss of one's innocence (the perception of nakedness) is instantaneous, but the moral implications of that event (the knowledge of good and evil) are acquired through experience, through learning over time, and a third-person perspective that helps one understand the experience (a perceived, constraining event) in terms of good and evil—although Morris doesn't put it quite this way. But anticipating the probability of disaster is not the same as understanding its moral significance. Disaster time is not the time of learning to face disaster; that is one major reason why ritual time and the time of discursive tradition (both of them times of learning) may be undermined, and why that undermining is itself an aspect of the great disaster.

It is undeniable that the freeing of secular reason has enabled spectacular accomplishments in science and technology, in humanistic knowledge, in the practical improvement of health and of living standards for many, as well as in artistic and literary creation. These accomplishments have often been "enchanting," but what disasters they might allow remains uncertain. The early period of European expansion in the making of the modern world was achieved at the cost of exceptional violence, typically expressed in and through a superior and continuously developing technology of war. The violence of civilization has not diminished today; on the contrary, its threat promises global catastrophe. The most significant aspect of secular reason that has brought us to where we are is a resourcefulness that employs increasing abstraction and calculation for formulating and resolving problems. Secular reason is not, of course, homogeneous, nor does it systematize all of contemporary life; it is even what reshapes, and what is therefore integral to, much contemporary religion. In acknowledging that modern life remains heterogeneous, I do not, however, wish to enter the well-known debates on "disenchantment." *That* Weberian notion seems to me to concede too much to a doctrinaire concept of secularity. A major point I want to emphasize is simply that in its paradigm of truth, or rationality, secular reason is ideally dependent on mathematization, something that offers both opportunities for knowledge as well as dangers. This is arguably the case even though resort to numbers was an important feature of much prescientific thinking and has been shown to be an important element of religious belief and practice from ancient Egypt to ancient China;[5] but it is precisely the metaphysics of number signs (as elaborated, for example, by Pythagoras) that differentiates the ancient preoccupation with number from secular reason's use of mathematics as a way of constructing passionless language, action, and thought.

The language of mathematics is essential not only to modern science but also to modern technology, modern governance, and the modern economy. The common assumption that scientific knowledge of the world is one thing (morally neutral) and its application in the world quite another (morally good or bad) is, in my view, profoundly mistaken. Scientific knowledge, experiment, and technology (or, as Anscombe put it: intention, and the means one uses to achieve that intention) are inextricably connected together, and so together embedded in social life. Without instrumental devices and methods, the process of practical demonstration required by the accumulation of scientific knowledge cannot be undertaken; and, conversely, progress in scientific knowledge is essential for the development of sophisticated techniques. Knowledge, as Adam discovered in Paradise, is the beginning of possible violence.

At any rate, no one really knows how to compute the outcome of several global crises—with their threat of mass extinction—that are now converging and pushing the world into uncharted territory. Confronted by the continually upgraded arsenal of nuclear missiles, where the United States refuses to renounce the "first strike" option, the likely prospect seems to be not the redemption of humanity through progress and reason but its horrendous collapse.[6] One of the many ironies now emerging is that those who speak in the name of secular modernity have long been sloganizing that *at last* "Man can now make his own history," and yet the history he has been making threatens the end of all life, not only his own.

I am reminded of the Babylonian epic *Gilgamesh*, which insists every happening has an end but that that limit is unknown. Thus, when the hero, Gilgamesh, is grieving over the death of his beloved companion, the wild man Enkidu, and searching for a way to escape his own death, an old man speaks to him as follows:

"You who were born of a goddess mother,
why do you grieve because of a mortal father?
How long does a building stand before it falls?
How long does a contract last? How long will brothers
share the inheritance before they quarrel?
How long does hatred, for that matter, last?
Time after time the river has risen and flooded.

The insect leaves the cocoon to live but a minute.
How long is the eye able to look at the sun?
From the very beginning nothing at all has lasted.
See how the dead and the sleeping resemble each other.
Seen together, they are the image of death.
The simple man and the ruler resemble each other.
The face of the one will darken like that of the other.
The Annunaki gathered in assembly;
Mammetum, Mother Goddess, she was with them.
There they established that there is life and death.
The day of death is set, though not made known."[7]

It is not only the life of man that must have an end. Gilgamesh
is told by the old man that the only certainty is the fall of everything that now exists, but when that end occurs (befalls) no one
can tell. According to secular, calculative reason, chance can be
tamed by probability theory, by minimizing loss and maximizing
gain. Yet that theory cannot determine when any given person's
death will happen or collective disaster befall.

In a movingly written and thought-provoking account of termi-
nal cancer patients, the anthropologist Abou Farman writes at
length about statistics, stressing that he is interested not in numbers as such (although, as he points out, enumeration is vital, in a
literal sense, to modern medicine) but in the fact that, with secularization, the patient's time to death—from life to nothingness—is
continuously being measured and estimated by the physician and
is reflected in the patient's feelings as her chances are continuously
re-estimated in this way.[8] Every event is an accident—a befalling—
and the time of future accidents, as Gilgamesh is told, cannot be
known. (Of course, if you leap from a high building, you will certainly die, but that *event* is accidental.)

So let us think about death and devastation first in nuclear war.
It is widely known that the relentless buildup of strategic nuclear

weapons has already witnessed many accidents and close calls. Some military analysts confidently claim that nuclear war between Russia and America was avoided during the Cold War era precisely because of the strategy known as mutually assured destruction, and therefore this strategy can be relied upon in the future. But this assumption is plausible only if human decisions are translatable into the secular language of rational choice theory. And as many have pointed out, rational choice theory employs a very impoverished language for understanding life as it is actually lived. More important, the fact that no nuclear war has taken place so far doesn't prove that it cannot happen in the future. Retired U.S. general Lee Butler once famously remarked that "mankind escaped the Cold War without a nuclear holocaust by some combination of diplomatic skill, blind luck and divine intervention, probably the latter in greatest proportion."[9] Should we continue to rely on divine intervention on our behalf? Or can we, as secular citizens, use our ability to calculate risk rationally?

In recent years the Pentagon has decided that America's enormous nuclear arsenal may not deter enemies precisely because the doctrine of mutually assured destruction *may* psychologically restrain the first use of weapons of mass destruction but that it does not preclude military attack. This has led strategists to argue that the conventional nuclear weapons are not a sufficient deterrent and that it is necessary therefore to develop low-yield tactical, nuclear munitions offering more flexible strike option than conventional nuclear warheads: a wonderful example of calculative reason. As critics have pointed out, however, this development would encourage military hostilities and greatly increase the danger of escalation leading to an all-out use of every available weapon.[10]

Death and devastation also threaten, but more slowly, through the results of climate change: One example of this is described in a recent report on the increasing deoxygenation of the oceans due not only to the warming of oceans resulting from climate change but

also to more direct human activity with more immediate consequences: the discharge into estuaries and coastal systems of the
nitrogen and phosphorus used as nutrients in industrial agriculture,
sewage, and the combustion of fossil fuels—several million square
kilometers are affected in this way. "Climate change exacerbates
oxygen decline in coastal systems through similar mechanisms as
those in the open ocean, as well as by increasing nutrient delivery
from watersheds that will experience increased precipitation.
Expansion of low-oxygen zones can increase production of N_2O, a
potent greenhouse gas; reduce eukaryote biodiversity; alter the
structure of food webs; and negatively affect food security and
livelihoods."[11]

Probability theory cannot predict the future: it can only raise
or lower anxiety about what might happen (befall). The buying
and selling of securities on the basis of probability theory has
become the basis for managing wealth for large sectors of the
population in modern society (leading to the poverty of even
greater numbers). But if probability theory is the way to measure
degrees of uncertainty, does this mean that it can give "reasonable men and women" assurance that global dislocation produced
by climate change can be avoided or mitigated in the future? Or
are we already in the midst of a disaster whose precise outcome
cannot be foreseen but should be feared?

Politicians and businessmen often speak of the great complexity
of the modern world. But shouldn't that sense of complexity temper one's confidence that the future and the past are within humanity's grasp? Of course, we can anticipate that using particular
means will lead to a particular end, but that is in the short term; in
the multiple temporalities in which our lives are entangled, exactly
when and how things will fall can't be predicted.[12] Contingencies
of textual scholarship, a continually reinterpretable historical
archive, mistakes in translation, and willful misinterpretation are
always part of the unanticipated results of action and among the

things that create uncertainty. The fact that there are many things in the past that we do not know now but will come to know only in the future (and that will therefore no longer be the future) renders the clear-cut line between an unchangeable past and an open future dubious—at least for long-term cases. Such accidents render the often-invoked attitude attributed to Gramsci ("pessimism of the intellect, optimism of the will") into an evasion. Intellect, the ability to see the world as it really is, to follow the methods of logic relentlessly, isn't entirely separable from will, desire, and sheer accident.[13] In global economies of complexity and states of enormous ambition, there is always the possibility of failure and, consequently, of resentment and accusations of betrayal.

This is something that seems to me to have been largely overlooked by both sides of the debate about Christianity as the historical origin of secularism: I find it surprising that those who translate Christian ideas into what they claim are equivalents in the modern world haven't addressed the question of human failure—failure of understanding, of action, of character, and of translation. But it is also something that those who reject a Christian genealogy of secularism have not attended to in their story of secular triumph. Failure is arguably a major insight of the so-called "world religions"—not only of Judaism, Christianity, and Islam but also of Hinduism, Buddhism, and Taoism. Of course, this is not to say that all these traditions have the same concept of failure or that what we understand in contemporary English by the word "failure" is to be found in essence in all languages.

In English we use the word "failure" in several senses, but in most cases there is the idea of a norm one has failed to achieve and of what is to count as success. Individual learning that requires practice as regulated by a discursive tradition typically goes through a sequence of failures. The failure I have in mind, however, is ignorance of the fact *that* one has failed, *that* one is ignorant of the true nature of one's actions and inactions—that humans forget they are essentially limited. According to many critics, political Islam has been unable to modernize their society or to provide viable alternatives to modernity, and it is their refusal to recognize this inability that constitutes its failure.[14] These critics are right in a sense but what they do not consider is whether, as promoters of "secularity" and "scientific knowledge" and "progress," they might not themselves be suffering from another failure: the failure to understand what human beings are capable and not capable of doing. The failure to understand the fatal consequences of how one acts, thinks, and feels in the world, the arrogance (hubris) in thinking one can act like a god, is what classical Greek dramatists saw as the essence of what they called tragedy. Early Christians also had a notion of failure that they called "pride of life": a lust for life in the world that promoted ignorance of human limits.[15] For many early Christians, such as hermits and monks, this required a literal disengagement with the world of sin and temptation. Although this view is different from the way most Christians today think of being involved in the world, it reminds us that personal pain as well as collective disaster emerges from certain kinds of obsession with worldly desires. But at any rate, neither the early Christian view nor the premodern Islamic views have the same sense as in the Greek sense of "tragedy."

I turn here to an idea of David Scott's, that evil—such as New World slavery and the Nazi Holocaust—are immoral events made up of acts that are irreparable. Evil, he writes, is not only unjustifiable: no form of compensation can ever rectify evil, and therefore justice can never reach it. The damage evil perpetrates is not only a matter of killing human beings but even more so of subjecting them to "social death." What the realization of having committed evil can do is the recognition that there now exists an irresolvable debt—a problem without a solution.[16]

What I find most striking about our contemporary attitudes is the widespread belief that every "problem" has a solution waiting to be discovered, sooner or later, and that therefore in principle nothing is impossible.[17] This view holds that the world—and our behavior in it—are in principle entirely knowable, and therefore predictable and controllable. But failure comes from the attempt to express the inexpressible, to explain the inexplicable, to do the impossible: poetry, as all good translators recognize, is the impossibility of capturing everything expressed in one language into the words of another. And that failure is not always a matter of conscious choice.

Today an important failure is our inability to create a form of collective life on this planet radically different from the liberal capitalist states in which we live. This failure seems to be due not to any lack of imagination or will: there are many highly intelligent and determined people who have presented visions of an attractive future. It has in great measure to do with inherited languages that disallow us from understanding our own institutional and psychological blockages and the resolution they call for.[18] Of course we can recognize and describe instances of cruelty and kindness, of betrayal and self-sacrifice, of suffering and happiness. But we don't have a language to speak adequately about the changes occurring in our collective life resulting from where we have gone wrong, and the things of value we may be losing irretrievably. This is not a matter of the familiar binary: the need for total revolution (what some have called "philosophies of despair," that is, a politics aimed at destroying the present and starting with new absolutes) as opposed to the possibilities of pragmatic reform (also described as "philosophies of hope," that is, of "a guiding commitment to the democratic possibility of modernity").[19] To develop such a language, one requires not only thought and speech but also practical conditions for a new form of life as well as time to meet and address danger.

In the final chapter of *The Origins of Totalitarianism*, Arendt observes that whenever governments became truly totalitarian (when they exercised sovereign power over the entire life of citizens), "they started to operate according to a system of values so radically different from all others, that none of our traditional legal, moral, or common sense utilitarian categories could any longer help us to come to terms with, or judge, or predict their course of action."[20] Our old language, she says, is no longer adequate.

Arendt did not think of totalitarianism simply as a historical episode but as the ever-present and growing danger to humanity:

> The conditions under which we exist today in the field of politics are indeed threatened [by totalitarian tendencies]. Their danger is not that they might establish a permanent world. Totalitarian domination, like tyranny, bears the seeds of its own destruction. Just as fear and the impotence from which fear springs are antipolitical principles and throw men into a situation contrary to political action, so loneliness and the logical–ideological deducing the worst that comes from it represent an anti-social situation and harbor a principle destructive for all human living-together.[21]

Even before the global crises with which we are all now familiar, Arendt foresaw the possibility of future disaster as a consequence of the loneliness (abstraction from human relations and human feeling) and the logical–ideological deducing the worst (obsessive use of abstract reason).

What might an adequate language for our time look like? I don't know, but it would not be the language of the state, or of capitalism.

When I referred in the past to Islamic traditions like *amr bi-l-ma'rūf* (which implies that mutual responsibility among friends includes persuading one another to do what is right and avoid what is wrong), I did so mainly to try to unthink our language of sovereign power, with its calculative, logical obsessions and the race to progress that that language invites us to join.[22] Unless one understands fully where one has come from and what one's collective life does to us, one cannot extricate oneself and look beyond the limitations of behavior and thought it imposes. I have no idea what such a language would look like or where it might lead. I am certainly not repeating the old claim that individual virtue is the foundation of all politics—although insisting that politics and ethics are quite separate seems to me unpersuasive. Here I merely suggest that perhaps resort to the discursive tradition of *amr bi-l-ma'rūf* may be one way of trying to think oneself *out* of our present failed language.

Of course in itself a new language unconnected with a form of life is not a guarantee of anything: From what I've said so far, it should be evident that I think *amr bi-l-ma'rūf* doesn't mean very much if friends do not share—at least in some measure—a form of life. To say that is almost redundant because friendship *is* a form of sharing, a mutual faith in each other's feelings and predispositions. But friendship is not part of the language of the modern state since the latter claims to repudiate any form of partiality; the language of friendship is therefore not merely independent of the state (like quietism) but can stand in opposition to it.[23] Friendship overlaps with faith, in the older sense of trust, which is why both are often recognized as varying in degree, intensity, and quality. A well-known *hadīth* (recorded tradition of the Prophet's life) cites the Prophet as saying: "If any among you sees something reprehensible [*munkaran*], let him change it by action [*bi-yadihi*]; if he cannot do that, then by his words [*fa-bi-lisānihi*]; if he cannot do that, then in his heart [*fa-bi-qalbihi*]—and that is the weakest form of faith [*wa dhālik ad'af-ul-imān*]."[24] If the inability to do or even say something in response to a wrong is the weakest form of faith (*imān*), then it is also a denial of friendship because critique by friends of one's belief and action is not purely intellectual; it affirms and extends the space of friendship (*sadāqa*), of loyalty (*istiqāma*)—the former also including the sense of truthfulness and the latter of uprightness as virtue—when the effort is made to appeal by persuasion as opposed to commanding on authority.

The prospects of persuasion depend not only on what is said, how it is said, and to whom but also on the *time* during which and at which the attempt takes place: the longer the interaction, the more that life is shared the greater the possibility of persuasion or compromise. It is, in any case, not unreasonable to retain a position that has apparently been refuted intellectually—or shown to be internally inconsistent—in the hope that ways will be found to restore and strengthen it later. Rational argument may sometimes persuade listeners/readers, but there is little evidence that it leads people with deeply held views and attitudes (including commitments to authority) to abandon them; on the contrary, powerful argument may lead to greater resistance to change.

But if language is activity in a shared form of life, then there are other ways of getting people to change. We know that the language of persuading others to change their ways takes forms other than reasoned argument and submission to "reason": shouting, abusing, cursing, joking, appealing, threatening, and so on. We often make things difficult for others in order to prod them to think and prepare for possible change. One does this by actions as well as words. Thus, civil disobedience and political boycott are forms of argument where life is shared but where roles and powers are not. Through civil disobedience or boycott, one criticizes those who wield power, asking them to change their wrongful behavior. The modern state typically refuses to recognize such action as argumentative language, calling it violence instead while disclaiming that description for its own use of force.

As psychoanalysis has taught us, the human capacity for willful ignorance is enormous. Therapies may sometimes be effective—but the reason for this is not the analysand's discovery of the "true" meaning of her experience. In psychoanalysis, "resistance" is a sign of self-deception. Acceptance of the sign's meaning toward which the analyst guides the patient is—so it has been plausibly argued—a consequence of indirect suggestions the former makes to the latter in accordance with her theory In order to be persuaded, the patient has to be, in some degree, suggestible to interpretations (even interpretations ostensibly made by herself).[25] If resistance is a sign to be interpreted, then suggestibility is a capacity that enables the analyst to help the patient.[26] But resistance in the form of civil disobedience is not a sign of self-deception.

How, if at all, we can adapt to unpredictable catastrophes in our life—collective as well as individual—is impossible to answer confidently. I find myself, like others today, in a condition more troubling than doubt and less reassuring than faith—especially the faith that the ideals of secular reason and the language in which it is expressed will ultimately resolve all problems and never create new, intractable ones.

NOTES

Introduction

1. Ludwig Wittgenstein, *On Certainty* (Oxford: Basil Blackwell, 1969), § 559.

2. Roman Jakobson, "On Linguistic Aspects of Translation," *Harvard Studies in Comparative Literature* 23, no. 1 (1959): 232–33.

3. Or "interpreter." See W. B. Gallie, *Peirce and Pragmatism* (Harmondsworth, Middlesex: Penguin, 1952).

4. Jakobson, "On Linguistic Aspects of Translation," 234.

5. Jakobson, 238.

6. Jakobson, 238.

7. *Gilgamesh*, trans. David Ferry (New York: Farrar, Straus and Giroux, 1992), xi.

8. Walter Benjamin, "The Task of the Translator," in W. Benjamin, *Illuminations*, edited and introduction by Hannah Arendt (New York: Schocken, 1969), 71.

9. Bronislaw Malinowski, *Argonauts of the Western Pacific: An Account of Native Enterprise and Adventure in the Archipeligoes of Melanesian New Guinea* (London: Routledge and Kegan Paul), 1922.

10. Daniel Ellsberg, *The Doomsday Machine: Confessions of a Nuclear War Planner* (New York: Bloomsbury, 2017), introduction, 67–69.

1. Secular Equality and Religious Language

1. Robert Skidelsky, "European Politics with an Islamic Face?" *Project Syndicate*, December 28, 2015, https://www.project-syndicate.org/col umnist/robert-skidelsky#Yk6PzkXhhQqhjdYt.99.
2. Larry Siedentop, *Inventing the Individual: The Origins of Western Liberalism* (Cambridge, Mass.: Harvard University Press, 2014), 333. The bitter conflict in Europe between secularists and the church over the last two hundred years, Siedentop claims,

> has distorted our understanding of the relationship between liberalism and Christianity. And that is because the proto-liberal beliefs which had developed within the church by the fifteenth century—the belief in moral equality and a range of natural rights, in a representative form of government and the importance of freer enquiry—only came together when they were deployed against the church's claim to have a right to "enforce" belief, with the help of secular rulers. (333)

3. "Jewish discourse provides us with the opportunity to integrate two different perspectives from which we should approach the question of secularism," writes Amnon Raz-Krakotzkin in a thoughtful and suggestive essay.

> The first is the historical analysis of the Jewish existence as a "problem" for modern secularism. The second perspective is provided by *Zionism as a project of westernization of the Jews, a process that in reality took place through an internalization of Christian perceptions of the Jews and their exile.* The secular Zionist, the figure that most represents the now fashionable "Judeo-Christian," has been constructed through a distinction from the East, from the Arab, and from the historical-exilic Jew. Zionism is an exceptional case, but one from which we can learn about the rule. Its analysis also reveals the potential inherent in the concept of exile for advancing an alternative option of secularity, one that itself demands a process of de-colonization.

Amnon Raz-Krakotzkin, "Secularism, the Christian Ambivalence Toward the Jews, and the Notion of Exile," in *Secularism in Question: Jews and Judaism in Modern Times*, ed. A. Joskowicz and E. B. Katz, 276–98 (Philadelphia: University of Pennsylvania Press, 2015), 276 (italics added).

4. Max Weber, "Science as a Vocation," in *From Max Weber: Essays in Sociology*, trans. and ed. H. H. Gerth and C. Wright Mills (London: Routledge and Kegan Paul, 1948), 139.

5. Hans Blumenberg, *The Legitimacy of the Modern Age* (1966; repr., Cambridge, Mass.: MIT Press, 1985).

6. Blumenberg, 9.

7. "One such translation that salvages the substance of a term is the translation of the concept of 'Man in the image of God' into the identical dignity of all men that deserves unconditional respect." Jürgen Habermas and Joseph Ratzinger, *The Dialectics of Secularization: On Reason and Religion* (San Francisco: Ignatius, 2006), 45. The duty of respect is the complement of the right to dignity.

8. See Hent Kalmo and Quentin Skinner, eds., *Sovereignty in Fragments: The Past, Present and Future of a Contested Concept* (Cambridge: Cambridge University Press, 2010).

9. See Joan Scott, "Secularism and Gender Equality," in *Religion, the Secular, and the Politics of Sexual Difference*, ed. L. Cady and T. Fessenden, 25–44 (New York: Columbia University Press, 2013).

10. On Marx and Mill, see Graeme Duncan, *Marx and Mill: Two Views of Social Conflict and Social Harmony* (Cambridge: Cambridge University Press, 1973). On the slave-holding political elite of Revolutionary America, see Domenico Losurdo, *Liberalism: A Counter-History* (London: Verso, 2011).

11. It is well known, for example, that John Stuart Mill, a founder of nineteenth-century liberalism, justified colonial authoritarianism by resorting to the notion of political immaturity, although colonialism and authoritarianism have now become antithetical to liberalism.

12. For a useful discussion of the differentiation of social institutions and domains, see José Casanova, *Public Religion in the Modern World* (Chicago: University of Chicago Press, 1994).

13. Michael Freeden's *Liberal Languages: Ideological Imaginations and Twentieth-Century Progressive Thought* (Princeton, N.J.: Princeton University Press, 2005) traces the historical overlap between liberal and nonliberal discourse but unfortunately has virtually nothing to say directly about the overlap of liberalization with secularization.

14. Louis Hartz, *The Liberal Tradition in America: An Interpretation of American Political Thought Since the Revolution* (New York: Harcourt, Brace, 1955).

15. Carl Schmitt pointed out that the equality of all humans and the inequality between citizen and alien together constitute an irresolvable contradiction in liberalism; citizenship is meaningless without an exclusive state, and liberalism requires a secular state. See Carl Schmitt, *The Crisis of Parliamentary Democracy* (Cambridge, Mass.: MIT Press, 1985 [1923]), especially preface to the second edition (1926).

16. Glen Newey, "Denial Denied: Freedom of Speech," *Amsterdam Law Forum* 2, no. 1 (2009).

17. Pierre Manent, *A World Beyond Politics? A Defense of the Nation State* (Princeton, N.J.: Princeton University Press, 2006), 14. A page later he asserts, "Because society is *represented* as a *divided* power, the citizen will be *powerless* to do much harm to one another." An astonishing instance of the power of representation.

18. Jean-Jacques Rousseau, *The Social Contract and Discourses* (London: Dent & Dutton, 1913), 16.

19. Manent, *World Beyond Politics*, 30.

20. Confident assumptions about the mutual exclusion of religion and the secular have been challenged at various levels. To take one example: Philip Gorski, in his excellent neo-Weberian study, *The Disciplinary Revolution: Calvinism and the Rise of the State of Early Modern Europe* (Chicago: University of Chicago Press, 2010), shows that Calvinism in early modern Europe was a critical part of the long genealogy of the modern secular state. This doesn't mean, of course, that what European imperial powers learned in their encounters with the non-European societies they conquered and administered in later centuries was insignificant for the development of the modern secular state. On the contrary, the modern state in Britain, especially, owes many crucial

aspects of its modernization to its position as the center of a global empire. For a brilliant account of how British experience of its Indian colony helped to shape the history of liberal thought, see Uday Singh Mehta's *Liberalism and Empire: A Study in Nineteenth-Century British Liberal Thought* (Chicago: University of Chicago Press, 1999). It remains a fact, nevertheless, that the major figures cited in histories of liberalism are European and that political initiative nearly always lay with the metropolitan center.

21. See *Oxford Historical Thesaurus*.
22. See Christopher J. Peters, "Equality Revisited," *Harvard Law Review* vol. 110, no. 5 (1997). But I argue in chapter 3 that the principle of equality is not necessarily vacuous when the abstract language of statistics is used.
23. Ronald Dworkin, "Liberalism," in Stuart Hampshire, T. M. Scanlon, Bernard Williams, Thomas Nagel, and Ronald Dworkin, ed., *Public and Private Morality* (Cambridge: Cambridge University Press, 1978), 127.
24. Ira Katznelson, "A Properly Defended Liberalism: On John Gray and the Filling of Political Life," *Social Research* 61, no. 3 (Fall 1994): 622.
25. See Philip Gleason, "Identifying Identity: A Semantic History," *Journal of American History* 69, no. 4 (1983).
26. See Michael Herzfeld, *The Social Production of Indifference: Exploring the Symbolic Roots of Western Bureaucracy* (Chicago: University of Chicago Press, 1992).
27. J. G. A. Pocock, "The Classical Theory of Deference," *American Historical Review* 81, no. 3 (1976): 522.
28. Albert O. Hirschman, *Exit, Voice, and Loyalty: Responses to Decline in Firms, Organizations, and States* (Cambridge, Mass.: Harvard University Press, 1981), 32.
29. See Samuel Moyn, *The Last Utopia; Human Rights in History* (Cambridge, Mass.: Harvard University Press, 2012).
30. See Jeremy Waldron, *Dignity, Rank, & Rights*, The Berkeley Tanner Lectures (Oxford, New York: Oxford University Press, 2012).
31. James Q. Whitman, "On Nazi 'Honour' and the New European 'Dignity,'" in *Darker Legacies of Law in Europe: The Shadow of National*

Socialism and Facism over Europe and Its Legal Traditions, ed. Christian Joerges and Navraj Singh Ghaleigh, 243–66 (Oxford: Hart, 2003), 247.

32. Whitman, 266.

33. Neal Ascherson, "Hopping in His Matchbox," *London Review of Books* 38, no. 11 (June 2, 2016). For an early similar argument, based on a doctoral dissertation, see David Schoenbaum, *Hitler's Social Revolution: Class and Status in Nazi Germany 1933–1939* (New York: Doubleday, 1966).

34. Umberto Eco, "Ur-Fascism," *New York Review of Books,* June 22, 1985. Samuel Moyn has persuasively argued that fear of the "communist threat" was crucial to the construction of a "personalist" alternative to both communism and capitalism in the modern development of human rights. See Samuel Moyn, *The Last Utopia: Human Rights in History* (Cambridge, Mass.: Harvard University Press, 2010).

35. "Mafīsh dimūqrātiya wa mafīsh mugtamaʿ intaqal ila-l-amām bidūn damm." See the YouTube video of the workshop organized by Namnam discussing the making of the new constitution after June 30, 2013 (halaqa niqāshiya lil-hayʾat al-injīlīyya hawl dastūr misr baʿd 30 yūnyū). Many middle-class workshops, Muslim and Christian, were held on this topic, especially in Cairo. http://www.youtube.com/watch?v=__rdetkbS_s.

36. Hannah Arendt, *On Violence* (New York: Harcourt, Brace & World, 1969), 25–26.

37. Carl Schmitt, *The Crisis of Parliamentary Democracy* (Cambridge, Mass.: MIT Press, 2000), 9.

38. See Eric Hobsbawm, *The Age of Empire, 1875–1914* (New York: Vintage, 1989).

39. See Aziz Rana, *The Two Faces of American Freedom* (Cambridge, Mass.: Harvard University Press, 2010).

40. Mahmood Mamdani makes this important argument with respect to colonial rule in Africa: "The exclusion that defined the specificity of civil society under colonial rule was that of race. Yet it is not possible to understand the nature of colonial power simply by focusing on the partial and exclusionary character of civil society. It requires, rather, coming to grips with the specific nature of power through which the population of subjects excluded from civil society was

actually ruled." Mahmood Mamdani, *Citizen and Subject: Contemporary Africa and the Legacy of Late Colonialism* (Princeton, N.J.: Princeton University Press, 1996), 15. Mamdani's point is that exclusion and differentiation were integral to the system of colonial rule and as such had a negative impact on the character of colonial revolt.

41. Michael Dunlop Young, *The Rise of the Meritocracy, 1870–2033: An Essay on Education and Equality* (London: Thames and Hudson, 1958).

42. Margaret Thatcher, Leaders Speech, Blackpool 1975, http://www .britishpoliticalspeech.org/speech-archive.htm?speech=121#banner. Emphasis added.

43. Michael Young, incidentally, coined the term "meritocracy." About half a century later he wrote some rueful comments on Tony Blair's appropriation of the idea of a meritocratic society from Margaret Thatcher. Michael Young, "Down with Meritocracy," *Guardian*, June 28, 2001.

44. Quoted in Jack Smith, "A Still Uncertain Election," *CounterPunch*, August 17, 2016. https://www.counterpunch.org/2016/08/17/a-still -uncertain-election/.

45. Young, *Rise of the Meritocracy*, 71.

46. It is true that responsibility may be attributed to an individual's behavior if it causes unintentional harm to another regardless of intent, but the absence of individual intention is generally taken to mean the absence of cruelty.

47. See, for example, Timothy Pachirat, *Every Twelve Seconds: Industrialized Slaughter and the Politics of Sight*, Yale Agrarian Studies Series (New Haven, Conn.: Yale University Press, 2011). A measure of cruelty is also inflicted on slaughterhouse workers by their conditions of work, shielded as they are from the public gaze (and political intervention): see Eric Schlosser, *Fast Food Nation: The Dark Side of the All-American Meal* (New York: Houghton Mifflin, 2001). On the further question of the enormous damage done to the global environment by industrialized agriculture—in particular by the ramifications of industrialized meat production—see Keegan Kuhn and Kip Anderson, *The Sustainability Secret: Rethinking Our Diet to Transform the World* (San Rafael, Calif.: Insight Editions, 2015).

48. For example, this account from Hialeah, Florida:

> In September 1987, the city council of Hialeah, Florida,
> passed an ordinance banning animal sacrifice. The spur was
> a newly proposed church, cultural center, and school run by
> devotees of Santaria, whose worship of their *orishas* often
> took sacrificial form. Not wanting to ban all animal killing—
> what would citizens eat?—the council defined the target of
> the ordinance precisely. The ruling aimed only at "sacrifice,"
> which it took to mean: "to unnecessarily kill, torment, tor-
> ture, or mutilate an animal in a public or private ritual or
> ceremony not for the primary purpose of food consump-
> tion." This definition was written to avoid the word "reli-
> gion." Instead, it offered an ostensibly neutral prohibition of
> *all* ritual or ceremonial animal killings, sacred and secular
> alike. The church protested, needless to say, claiming an
> infringement of its First Amendment free exercise rights.
> But when the court for the southern district of Florida heard
> the case, it agreed with the city fathers and insisted that there
> were no grounds for a religious exception to this "absolute
> prohibition on ritual sacrifice." As the Humane Society
> argued, Hialeah did not ban just religious sacrifice; rather,
> "animal sacrifice is banned altogether."

    Jonathan Sheehan, "Sacrifice Before the Secular," *Representations* 105,
    no. 1 (Winter 2009): 12–36, at 12.

49. See, for example, Michael Walzer, *Just and Unjust Wars: A Moral Argu-
    ment with Historical Illustrations* (New York: Basic Books, 1977).

50. "The understanding of tolerance in pluralistic societies with a liberal
    constitution demands that in their dealings with unbelievers and
    those of different faiths, believers should grasp that they must rea-
    sonably expect that the dissent they encounter will go on existing; at
    the same time, however, a liberal political culture expects that unbe-
    lievers, too, will grasp the same point in their dealings with believ-
    ers." Habermas and Ratzinger, *Dialectics of Secularization*, 50.

51. Maeve Cooke, "A Secular State for a Postsecular Society? Postmeta-physical Political Theory and the Place of Religion," *Constellations* 14, no. 2 (2007): 234–35.

52. Charles Larmore, "Political Liberalism," *Political Theory* 18, no. 3 (1990): 347–48.

53. According to John Rawls, the most coherent model of liberalism ("the original position") presupposes two principles of equality: (1) that everyone has equal basic rights and freedoms—especially political freedoms—and (2) that different official positions defining formal inequalities in society must themselves be open to all, and that social and economic inequalities must be to the benefit of the least advantaged members of society. The first principle, familiar from classical liberalism, is thus concerned with the metaphysics of equality and the second, with equality of opportunity as an ideal. The distributary element in the second principle has generated much criticism from other liberals. Perhaps the most significant criticism of Rawls is that his conception of liberalism makes sense only if there is a single uncontested vision of the good life—a single theory of what human beings ought to be like. John Rawls, *Political Liberalism* (New York: Columbia University Press, 1993).

54. Jürgen Habermas, "Faith and Knowledge," in *The Frankfurt School on Religion: Key Writings by Major Thinkers*, ed. Eduardo Mendieta, 327–38 (New York: Routledge, 2005), 335–36; emphasis added.

55. T. S. Eliot, "Virgil and the Christian World" [1951], in *On Poetry and Poets* (New York: Farrar, Straus and Cudahy, 1957), 137.

56. Dennis Potter, *Seeing the Blossom: Two Interviews, a Lecture and a Story* (London: Faber and Faber), 57.

57. September 11, 2001, is thought by many to signal the beginning of a new form of global violence in which a particular religious tradition (Islam) is shown to be incapable of joining modernity. One cannot help wondering, however, whether the relative silence on the bombing of Hiroshima and Nagasaki, which really *did* initiate a new era—the era of looming nuclear devastation of life, possibly all life—has some significance for our conception of modernity. See John Dower,

The Violent American Century: War and Terror Since World War II (Chicago: Haymarket Books, 2017).

58. Jürgen Habermas, "A Conversation about God and the World," in *Religion and Rationality: Essays on Reason, God, and Modernity,* ed. Eduardo Mendieta (Cambridge, Mass.: Polity Press, 2002), 148–49.

59. The historical Christian view of Judaism is reflected partly in Siedentop's reference to "St Paul's contrast between 'Christian liberty' and observance of the Jewish law." Siedentop, *Inventing the Individual,* 333.

60. "Our language," Wittgenstein wrote, "can be seen as an ancient city, a maze of little streets and squares, of old and new houses, and of houses with additions from various periods; and this surrounded by a multitude of new boroughs with straight regular streets and uniform houses." Ludwig Wittgenstein, *Philosophical Investigations* (Oxford: Basil Blackwell, 1953), PI 18. The buildings exhibit different styles and fulfill different functions; some exist in various stages of completion or dismantling, some reflect the intentions of planners and some shape those intentions—often unconsciously. The city's boundaries can be specified with precision only for some purposes. This is why translation from one language to another often encounters incommensurabilities. Even renderings from poetry into prose in the same language may end up mutilating the original. The idea of language as a system is an abstraction—useful for some purposes but more often than not misleading.

61. Walter Benjamin, "The Task of the Translator," in *Illuminations,* ed. Hannah Arendt, 69–82 (New York: Schocken Books, 1969), 80–81.

62. Scott, "Secularism and Gender Equality," 28.

63. Scott, 28.

64. *Rapport au Président de la République: Commission de réflexion sur l'application du principe de laïcité dans la République,* Remis le 11 décembre 2003, (http://www.ladocumentationfrancaise.fr). The report has also been published in book form as *Laïcité et République, Commission présidée par BERNARD STASI* (Paris: La Documentation française, 2004).

65. Talal Asad, "Trying to Understand French Secularism," in *Political Theologies: Public Religions in a Post-Secular World,* ed. Hent de Vries, 494–526 (New York: Fordham University Press, 2006).

66. Ghislaine Hudson, in an interview with a group of young people published as "Laïcité. Une loi nécessaire ou dangereuse?" *Le Monde*, December 11, 2003.

67. See *Laïcité et République*, 102–3.

68. The paragraph that follows is drawn from Talal Asad, *Genealogies of Religion: Discipline and Reasons of Power in Christianity and Islam* (Baltimore: Johns Hopkins University Press, 2009), 125.

2. Translation and the Sensible Body

1. Lamin Sanneh, *Translating the Message: The Missionary Impact on Culture* (Maryknoll, N.Y.: Orbis, 1989), 3. Homi Bhabha's well-known account of what he calls "evangelical colonialism" (*The Location of Culture* [London: Routledge, 1994], 34) is the kind of argument against which Sanneh offers a defense.

2. Sanneh, *Translating the Message*, 8.

3. I have discussed critically the frequently used term "sacred" in Talal Asad, *Formations of the Secular: Christianity, Islam, Modernity* (Stanford, Calif.: Stanford University Press, 2003), 30–37. My argument, however, is not that "sacred" has no sense in any context but that it is not an explanatory term.

4. See Brett Wilson, *Translating the Qur'an in an Age of Nationalism: Print Culture and Modern Islam in Turkey* (London: Oxford University Press, Institute of Ismaili Studies, 2014).

5. Jacques Derrida, "Above All, No Journalists!" in *Religion and Media*, ed. Hent de Vries and Samuel Weber, 56–93 (Stanford, Calif.: Stanford University Press, 2001), 88.

6. There are, of course, critical questions—on which there is disagreement within the Islamic tradition—regarding the criteria by which one validly identifies passages calling for special explication, and by which one distinguishes "evident" from "hidden" meanings in the divine text (*zāhir* and *bātin*).

7. See Ismet Binark and Halit Eren, *World Bibliography of Translations of the Meanings of the Holy Qur'an* (Istanbul: IRCICA, 1986). The various translations reveal different motives for undertaking it.

8. Baber Johansen, *Contingency in a Sacred Law: Legal and Ethical Norms in the Muslim Fiqh* (Leiden: Brill, 1999), 65–66.

9. See Travis Zadeh, *The Vernacular Qur'an: Translation and the Rise of Persian Exegesis* (Oxford: Oxford University Press, 2012).

10. "Say: 'If the sea were ink for the words of my Lord, the sea itself would run dry before the words of my Lord had run dry, even if We provided its like to replenish it.'" Qur'an 18:108.

11. R. G. Collingwood, *The Principles of Art* (Oxford: Clarendon, 1938), 162.

12. R. Solomon, *The Passions: Emotions and the Meaning of Life* (Indianapolis: Hackett, 1976).

13. In his fascinating monograph *From Passions to Emotions* (Cambridge: Cambridge University Press, 2003), Thomas Dixon has traced the emergence of "emotion" as a secular psychological category.

14. T. S. Eliot, "The Metaphysical Poets," in *Selected Essays*, 3rd ed. (London: Faber and Faber, 1951). But in a perceptive article, F. M. Kuna argues that Eliot's influential notion of the dissociation of sensibility was *a modern theory* about seventeenth-century poetry rather than its reality:

    > The simple truth seems to be that critics who isolate Eliot's phrase from its context in order to apply it to a theory of their own are bound to involve themselves in a certain confusion. It is all too easy to forget that most of Eliot's criticism is, after all, "workshop-criticism." When Eliot wrote his essays he was thinking rather of his own poetry and of the re-evaluation of the past by a modern mind than of an objective appraisal of earlier poetry.

    F. M. Kuna, "T. S. Eliot's Dissociation of Sensibility and the Critics of Metaphysical Poetry," *Essays in Criticism* 13, no. 3 (1963): 241.

15. See Margreta de Grazia, "The Secularization of Language in the Seventeenth Century," *Journal of the History of Ideas* 41, no. 2 (1980): 319–29. doi:10.2307/2709464.

16. Peter Dear, *Discipline and Experience: The Mathematical Way in the Scientific Revolution* (Chicago: University of Chicago Press, 1995), 11–12. See

also Lorraine Daston's *Classical Probability in the Enlightenment* (Princeton, N.J.: Princeton University Press, 1988), in which she traces the kinds of everyday experience (e.g., aleatory contracts and variable conditions of doubt) that were translated into mathematics in the history of probability theory.

17. See *Historical Thesaurus of the English Dictionary*.

18. And yet, see Qur'an 2:115. I use the term "grammar" here following Wittgenstein, for whom the term refers not simply to the formal rules of "proper" syntactic constructions in natural language utterances but to the system of usages that permit some statements within particular ways of life and not others to make sense. Thus: "our investigation . . . is directed not towards phenomena, but, as one might say, towards the '*possibilities*' of phenomena. We remind ourselves, that is to say, of the *kind of statement* that we make about phenomena." Ludwig Wittgenstein, *Philosophical Investigations*, part I, sec. 90 (Oxford: Blackwell, 1953). Wittgenstein's term, "grammar," takes the rule-governed character of language to be not a calculus but a game.

19. "And when the lesson is memorized, students often wash the boards and then drink the water, bringing the Word into their bodies as the Qur'an was poured into Muhammad, the Walking Qur'an." Rudolph T. Ware III, *The Walking Qur'an: Islamic Education, Embodied Knowledge, and History in West Africa* (Chapel Hill: University of North Carolina Press, 2014), 10.

20. Indigenous conceptions of the body—of which visible indisposition is merely one condition—need to be brought in here if one is to understand better the cultural assumptions underlying the motivation for condemning or supporting practices in particular traditions. The word "superstition" (*khurāfa*) has a long history intimately connected with the word "religion" as well as "science." See Emile Benveniste, *Indo-European Language and Society*, trans. Elizabeth Palmer (Coral Gables, Fla.: University of Miami Press, 1973), 516–28.

21. In a recent piece, Ebrahim Moosa writes: "when 'Aisha, the Prophet Muhammad's wife is asked about his character she promptly replies, according to Muslim tradition, that his character was the embodiment of the Qur'an. In fact she said his character was identical to the

requirements of the revelation; or put differently, she can be con-
strued as having said that his character was attuned to revelation."
Entry on "Qur'ānic Ethics" in *Oxford Handbook of Qur'anic Studies*, edited
by Muhammad Abdel Haleem and Mustafa Shah (forthcoming).

22. The Maliki school, the earliest of the four Sunni schools, sometimes
gives precedence to "the custom of Medina" as against hadith on the
grounds that the latter is the recorded report of a single event whereas
the practice of the community of Medina, where the Prophet lived
in the latter part of his life, represented a living tradition embodied
in action. See Yasin Dutton, *The Origins of Islamic Law: The Qur'an, the
Muwatta' and Madinan 'Amal*, 2nd rev. ed. (London: RoutledgeCurzon,
2002).

23. This story is recounted in what is now considered a classic: Werner
Jaeger's *Early Christianity and Greek Paideia* (Cambridge, Mass: Harvard
University Press, 1995). In this book, Jaeger approaches *paideia* as a
comprehensive philosophy or a literary culture that has an educative
function: "As the Greek paideia consists of the entire corpus of Greek
literature, so the Christian paideia is the Bible" (92). The preoccupation with textual meaning led the early theorists of this tradition
to specify several levels of sense to be conveyed in Biblical education.

24. See Sanneh, *Translating the Message*, 274–75.

25. This goes beyond the so-called Abrahamic religions. See Garth
Fowden's *Before and After Muhammad: The First Millennium Refocused*
(Princeton, N.J.: Princeton University Press, 2014). Marshall Hodg-
son's classic *The Venture of Islam: Conscience and History in a World Civilization*, 3 vols. (Chicago: University of Chicago Press, 1974), especially
the first two volumes, are of course indispensable for understanding
the interactions between Islam and other traditions within a much
wider space than the Eastern Mediterranean. For example, when the
Seljuq Turks converted to Islam in the tenth century and established
a large empire from central Asia through to the Middle East, the
Islamic tradition was exposed to Buddhism, Shamanism, Man-
ichaeism, and Nestorian Christianity. It does not follow from this,
of course, that each tradition is *merely* the product of interaction with
others.

26. Michael Sells, in his book on pagan, Christian, and Islamic mystical discourses, has put it well: "Rather than focusing upon the textual 'borrowings' of one tradition or another, it seems more profitable to see these traditions as competing within a partially shared intellectual and symbolic world, defining themselves in conversation with one another and against one another." Michael Sells, *Mystical Languages of Unsaying* (Chicago: University of Chicago Press, 1994), 5. This perspective is far more illuminating than the Orientalist preoccupation with so-called foreign origins in religious traditions because it attends to translation as a conversation.

27. See Pierre Hadot, *Philosophy as a Way of Life* (Oxford: Blackwell, 1995).

28. Jean Leclerc, "Pour l'histoire de l'expression 'philosophie chrétienne,'" *Mélanges de Science Religieuse* 9 (1952): 221–22.

29. See Ghazālī, *Ihyā*, vol. 4, p. 567.

30. Thus, as with the Ten Commandments, "Thou shalt not kill!" cannot be converted into a conditional: "Thou may kill only if a greater good is achieved by killing." This was known in medieval casuistry as the principle of the double effect.

31. Including what medieval writers in Islam, Christianity, and Judaism called "common sense" (*al-hiss al-mushtarak*), an integrative function, not to be confused with what "common sense" has come to mean today. See Harry A. Wolfson, "The Internal Senses in Latin, Arabic, and Hebrew Philosophical Texts," *Harvard Theological Review* 28, no. 2 (1935): 69–133. Much of the groundwork for this problem has been laid by Daniel Heller-Roazen's *The Inner Touch: The Archaeology of a Sensation* (New York: Zone, 2009).

32. For example: "And so appetite for food is a kind of will," *fa idhan shahwat al-ta'ām ahad durūb al-irādāt*. Abu-Hamid al-Ghazālī, *Ihyā 'Ulūm al-Dīn*, vol. 4 (Cairo: al-Quds, 2012), 173.

33. The latter, incidentally, became significant in the fifteenth century and, therefore, much later than the practice of imitating the Prophet among Muslims.

34. The distinction between theoretical and practical knowledge, revived in modern Anglophone philosophy by Elizabeth Anscombe, has its roots in Aristotelianism and is found in the Islamic, Judaic, and

Christian traditions of virtue ethics that inherited it. Her most brilliant work is *Intention* (Oxford: Blackwell, 1957); several of her thought-provoking essays, especially "Modern Moral Philosophy" (1958), "Authority in Morals" (1960), and "War and Murder" (1961), have been collected in *Ethics, Religion and Politics* (Oxford: Blackwell, 1981).

35. Hadot, *Philosophy as a Way of Life*, 211. Subsequent critics have accused Foucault, as Hadot did, of a relapse into Romanticism, but Behrooz Ghamari-Tabrizi has convincingly argued that Foucault's later work was fruitfully affected by his response to the Islamic Revolution in Iran. See Behrooz Ghamari-Tabrizi, *Foucault in Iran: Islamic Revolution after the Enlightenment* (Minneapolis: University of Minnesota Press, 2016).

36. S. Collini, "The Idea of 'Character' in Victorian Political Thought," in *Transactions of the Royal Historical Society*, fifth ser., no. 55 (London: Royal Historical Society, 1985), 38.

37. On the icon for believing Christians, see Rowan Williams, *Lost Icons: Reflections on Cultural Bereavement* (London: Moorhouse, 2000).

38. See E. E. Evans-Pritchard, *Theories of Religion* (Oxford: Oxford University Press, 1965), 44–45. In his classic study of prayer, Marcel Mauss (1909; *On Prayer*, trans. by Susan Leslie, ed. by W. S. F. Pickering [New York: Berghahn Books, 2008]) makes a fundamental distinction between prayer rituals and incantation rituals, where the latter refers to an essentially instrumental action and the former to a social relation. This distinction clearly derives from the Durkheimian interest in tracing the supposed evolution of religion, but both prayer ("religion") and incantation ("magic") are intentional, albeit with different objectives, and according to Mauss both are found together.

39. Stanley Tambiah, *A Performative Approach to Ritual* (London: British Academy, 1981), 132.

40. Caroline Humphrey and James Laidlaw, *The Archetypal Actions of Ritual: A Theory of Ritual Illustrated by the Jain Rite of Worship* (Oxford: Clarendon Press, 1994).

41. Humphrey and Laidlaw, 88–89.

42. Humphrey and Laidlaw, 135.

43. See Franz Brentano, *Psychology from an Empirical Standpoint* (1874; repr. London: Routledge, 1995).

44. See also Ibn Taymiyya's critique of Greek logic because and to the extent that it requires concepts be carefully defined for sound thought. His position, incidentally, is not to be confused with ordinary language philosophy. See Taqi ad-Dīn Ibn Taymiyya, *Jahd al-Qarīha fi Tajrīd an-Nasīha*, summarized by al-Hāfiz Jalāl ad-Dīn as-Suyūti (Beirut: Maktabat al-'Asriyya, 2009).

45. Marcel Mauss, *On Prayer*, trans. Susan Leslie (1909; repr. New York: Berghahn, 2003), 21, 22.

46. The Arabic name of Hebron, incidentally, is *khalīl* because Abraham is believed to be buried there.

47. Paul R. Powers, *Intent in Islamic Law: Motive and Meaning in Medieval Sunni Fiqh* (Leiden: Brill, 2006), 9–10.

48. Powers, 58.

49. Powers, 59, italics added

50. Jackson writes:

> In the case of the five daily prayers, what al-Qarāfi wants to protect is . . . the right to offer prayer in a fashion perhaps unique by comparison with others, e.g., the right to pray without reciting the *basmalah* or the entire Opening Chapter, issues over which there is disagreement among the schools of law. Regarding these issues, al-Qarāfi wants to insist that government has not the authority to intervene and impose any particular modality of compliance upon the community.

> Sherman A. Jackson, *Islamic Law and the State: The Constitutional Jurisprudence of Shihāb al-Dīn al-Qarāfi* (Leiden: Brill, 1996), 203.

51. Lena Salaymeh, "Taxing Citizens: Socio-Legal Constructions of Late Antique Muslim Identity," *Islamic Law and Society* 23, no. 4 (2016): 333–367.

52. Salaymeh observes:

> The Islamic charity tax does not neatly correspond to the modern bifurcation between religion and the secular. It is only

when we displace the charity tax from the modern category of religion and place it within its historical surroundings that we can appreciate its multiple meanings. Many late antique legal authorities required minors—but not slaves—to pay the charity tax because citizenship, rather than belief, triggered the obligation to pay. Still, the charity tax is not simply a "mixing" of the for-the-divine and the for-the-polity. Instead, it is a manifestation of the inextricable connection between Islamic law and governance (Salaymeh, 354).

53. For an interesting account of contemporary Islamic attitudes to *zakāt*, see Cihan Tuğal's study account of charity organizations in Egypt and Turkey: *Caring for the Poor: Islamic and Christian Benevolence in a Liberal World* (New York: Routledge, 2017).

54. Elizabeth Anscombe, "War and Murder: The Use of Violence by Rulers," in *Ethics, Religion and Politics*, 58–59.

55. Anscombe, 59.

56. Wittgenstein, *Philosophical Investigations*, sec. 202.

57. See Antony Flew and Godfrey Vesey, *Agency and Necessity* (Oxford: Basil Blackwell, 1987), 7; and John Cottingham, *Philosophy and the Good Life: Reason and the Passions in Greek, Cartesian and Psychoanalytic Ethics* (Cambridge: Cambridge University Press, 1998), 101.

58. See Sheri Fink, "Las Vegas Gunman's Brain Will Be Scrutinized for Clues to the Killing," *New York Times*, October 26, 2017.

59. This is apparent in the historical usages recorded for the word "motive" in the *Oxford English Dictionary*: "That which 'moves' or induces a person to act in a certain way; a desire, fear, or other emotion, or a consideration of reason, which influences or tends to influence a person's volition; also often applied to a contemplated result or object the desire of which tends to influence volition. Writers of the 17–18th c. commonly speak of acting *on* a motive; the usual preposition now is *from*, though occasionally *with* or *for* is employed."

60. Incidentally, despite this famous mechanical model, it has been argued that in his later writings Descartes began developing an

ethics that transcends a simple dualism between mind and matter based on an anthropology in which the role of feelings is central. See Cottingham, *Philosophy and the Good Life*, 87n52.

61. "When, from 1949 to 1953, a British Royal Commission studied the topic of capital punishment, fully one-fourth of its final report concerned the insanity defense and the relationship between mental illness, crime, and punishment." Thomas Maeder, *Crime and Madness: The Origins and Evolution of the Insanity Defense* (New York: Harper and Row, 1985), 74. Maeder has an account of the complicated history of the insanity defense in England and America. For an account of the eighteenth-century case that formally established the "knowing right from wrong" principle, see Richard Moran, *Knowing Right from Wrong: The Insanity Defense of Daniel McNaughtan* (New York: Free Press, 1981). Janet Ann Tighe has written a fascinating doctoral dissertation entitled "A Question of Responsibility: The Development of American Forensic Psychiatry, 1838–1930" (University of Pennsylvania, 1983), that is, unfortunately, still not published.

62. Lori Branch, *Rituals of Spontaneity* (Waco, Texas: Baylor University Press), 2–3.

63. Branch, 6.

64. Branch, 22.

65. The most famous example in anthropology of this point of view is Eric Hobsbawm and Terence Ranger, eds., *The Invention of Tradition* (Cambridge: Cambridge University Press, 1983).

66. Ahmed Fekry Ibrahim, "The Sunni Legal Tradition: An Overview of Pluralism, Formalism, and Reform," in *Sustainable Diversity in Law: Essays in Memory of H. Patrick Glenn*, ed. Helge Dedek (Oxford: Oxford University Press, 2018).

67. See Aron Zysow, *The Economy of Certainty: An Introduction to the Typology of Islamic Legal Theory* (Atlanta: Lockwood, 2013).

68. The relevant passage in the original reads: *'inna al-umama jamī'ahum min 'ahl al-'ulūmi wa-l-maqālāt wa 'ahl al-a'māl wa-ssinā'āt ya'rifūna al-umūr allatī yahtājūn 'ila ma'rifatihā wa yuhaqqiqūna mā yu'ānūnahu min al-'ulūm wa-l-a'māl*

min ghayr takallam bi-hadd [mantiqiy]. Jalal al-Din al-Suyuti's abridged version (*Juhd al-qariha fi tajrid al-nasiha* [Beirut: al-Maktabat al-'Asriyya, 2009], 29) of Ibn Taymiyya's book, *Nasihat ahl al-iman fi al-radd 'ala mantiq al-yunan.* Suyuti's abridgment has been translated by Wael Hallaq as *Ibn Taymiyya Against the Greek Logicians* (Oxford: Clarendon, 1993). See, esp., 7. In my transliteration of the relevant passage I have added *mantiqiy* ("logical") after *hadd* ("definition")—but in square brackets—because it appears thus in a collection of extracts from the voluminous work of Ibn Taymiyya: Abdur-Rahman bin Nasir al-Sa'di, *Tariq al-wasul ila al-'ilm al-ma'mul* (Alexandria: Dar al-Basirah, n.d.).

69. "While the diversity of languages constitutes a great cultural treasure, it also serves as an obstacle to the primary function of language, which is communication." Willard G. Oxtoby, "'Telling in Their Own Tongues': Old and Modern Bible Translations as Expressions of Ethnic Cultural Identity," *Concilium,* 1995.

3. Masks, Security, and the Language of Numbers

1. Mauss's essay was given as a lecture to a British audience in French in 1938. The original was published posthumously in a collection entitled *Marcel Mauss: Sociologie at anthropologie,* ed. Claude Levi-Strauss (Paris: Presses Universitaires de France, 1960), 333–62.

2. Abou Farman has explored some of the tensions underlying these and other dualities constituting modern conceptions of the body in an important article, "Speculative Matter: Secular Bodies, Minds, and Persons," *Cultural Anthropology* 28, no 4, (2013).

3. An eminent anthropologist who has been influenced by Wittgenstein is Veena Das.

4. Clifford Geertz, *The Interpretation of Cultures* (New York: Basic Books, 1973), 10.

5. Maurice Bloch, ed., *Political Language and Oratory in Traditional Society* (London: Academic Press, 1972); and Maurice Bloch, "Symbols, Song, Dance and Features of Articulation," *European Journal of Sociology* 15, no. 1 (May 1974): 54–81.

6. "What gets said, or rather cannot be said, is laid down by this polite, respectful behavior, both linguistic and non-linguistic," writes Bloch. "In these formal interactions if you stay within the code you can only listen in silence and allow a pause to elapse afterwards— which in fact means yes. The speaker and hearer have slipped into a highly structured situation which contains the hierarchical situation which only allows for a one-way relationship." Bloch, *Political Language*, 9.

7. "In the case of political oratory, we saw that the sign and the tool of traditional authority was formalised communication and that in the case of religious rituals this formalisation is pushed even further." Bloch, "Symbols, Song, Dance," 77.

8. Bloch, *Political Language*, 13. Bloch, incidentally, uses "code," "language," and "speech act" interchangeably. But a speech act can't be impoverished or rich, it can only be what J. L. Austin called "happy" or "unhappy"—that is, appropriately performed or not, "taking" or "miscarrying." A code can only be efficient or inefficient for producing particular kinds of message. The all-purpose word "language" is far too wide here: to speak of a language being "impoverished" may refer either to the ability of the user or to the possibilities of a use. In the latter case, one has to define the scope of a conventional language (which in this context means a vocabulary and its usages) and the new purpose for which it is inadequate. This is precisely what Bloch doesn't do.

9. A difficulty with this part of Bloch's thesis is the lack of clarity in his notion of formalization. There are at least two quite different senses in which Bloch uses it. First, there is the sense in which linguistic and paralinguistic options available to speakers can be predicted in given situations; here more "formal" would mean predictable with greater probability. The idea of predictable behavior is what induces Bloch to speak of constraint. Yet every appropriate formulation of a sentence involves a sequence of choices whose range necessarily narrows as it approaches its end. In this very banal sense it is true that when the sentence is properly completed it no longer has a linguistic

potential *as that sentence* because it has just been realized. But this doesn't mean that predictability here—whether used in religious liturgy or in political oratory (or where both are merged)—indicates impoverished language, or a narrowing potentiality for communication: It cannot therefore be said that ritual constraint is the foundation of traditional authority, whether that is labeled "religious" or "secular." The second sense of "formality" in Bloch stands in simple contrast to "informality," the one being defined in terms of the other. In this latter sense, neither term is directly correlated with the range of options available—for example, that writing is "formal" and speech "informal" doesn't therefore mean that the former must have fewer linguistic options available to it. In other words, both "formality" and "informality" in speech may be indices of social relations, roles, and so on, and as such both are socially significant "forms." In this signifying sense, speech is of course merely one modality of "forms": gesture, dress, material objects, and so on, are also recognizable forms or "signs."

10. This is a collective work, although Seligman appears to be the primary author, so I shall refer for convenience to him only. Adam B. Seligman, Robert P. Weller, Michael J. Puett, and Bennett Simon, *Ritual and Its Consequences: An Essay on the Limits of Sincerity* (Oxford: Oxford University Press, 2008).

11. Seligman et al., 7–11.

12. Ulrich Beck, *World at Risk* (Cambridge: Polity Press, 2009).

13. Ian Hacking wrote an excellent history of statistics entitled *The Taming of Chance* (Cambridge: Cambridge University Press, 1990); a more significant title might have been *The Taming of Uncertainty*.

14. Erving Goffman, *The Presentation of Self in Everyday Life* (Edinburgh, U.K.: University of Edinburgh, Social Sciences Research Centre, 1956).

15. Shortly after the appearance of Goffman's book, Anselm Strauss published *Mirrors and Masks: The Search for Identity* (Glencoe, Ill.: Free Press, 1959), which was widely read as an introduction—and contribution—to the burgeoning literature on "symbolic interactionism."

16. Goffman, *Presentation of Self*, 2–3.

17. Goffman, 5.

18. Alvin W. Gouldner, *The Coming Crisis of Western Sociology* (London: Heinemann, 1970), 387.

19. Skinner makes his argument for a different conception of political morality in Machiavelli's writing (as opposed to his alleged immorality) in *The Foundations of Modern Political Thought* (Cambridge: Cambridge University Press, 1978), 1:128–38. The specific reference to Leo Strauss on Machiavelli as an example of what Skinner considers to be a typical misunderstanding of Machiavelli occurs on page 137.

20. This is clearly an awkward translation. Quentin Skinner makes better sense, as follows: "few are in a position to come in close touch." Quentin Skinner *The Foundations of Modern Political Thought*, vol. 1, *The Renaissance* (Cambridge: Cambridge University Press, 1978), 132.

21. Niccolò Machiavelli, *The Prince* (London: Oxford University Press, 1952), 68 and 79.

22. Skinner, *Foundations of Modern Political Thought*, 1:137.

23. Skinner, 134–35.

24. In Latin, incidentally, the word *"sponte"* means "voluntarily, freely." *Oxford English Dictionary*.

25. There are numerous publications that have made important contributions to this account. Apart from the excellent *Rituals of Spontaneity: Sentiment and Secularism from Free Prayer to Wordsworth* by Lori Branch (Waco, Texas: Baylor University Press, 2006), I have found the following helpful: Stephen Greenblatt, *Renaissance Self-Fashioning: From More to Shakespeare* (Chicago: Chicago University Press, 1980); Adela Pinch, *Strange Fits of Passion: Epistemologies of Emotion, Hume to Austen* (Stanford, Calif.: Stanford University Press, 1996); Lawrence Klein and Anthony La Volpa, eds., *Enthusiasm and Enlightenment in Europe, 1650–1850* (San Marino, Calif.: Huntington Library Press, 1998); and Scott Paul Gordon, *The Power of the Passive Self in English Literature, 1640–1770* (Cambridge: Cambridge University Press, 2002).

26. Jean-Jacques Rousseau, *The Social Contract and Discourses* (London: Everyman Edition, 1913), 28.

27. During the eighteenth century, the expression of powerful emotion (then called "enthusiasm") was regarded by Enlightenment critics as a defining character of religion; in our day liberal theorists describe enthusiasm as something overcome by Enlightenment reason in civilized politics. But enthusiasm has continued to be part of secular projects—especially in the formation of national identity and the search for individuals who are suspected of betraying it.

28. Wilson's December 7, 1915, Third Annual Message to Congress address can be found at the American Presidency Project website, http://www.presidency.ucsb.edu/ws/index.php?pid=29556.

29. Hannah Arendt, *The Origins of Totalitarianism*, new ed. (New York: Harcourt Brace Jovanovich, 1968), 471.

30. One form of treason in thought is what Stanley Cavell has called "disowning knowledge," arguing, in a persuasive analysis of *Othello*, that the real treason depicted in that play is not Desdemona's suspected infidelity but Othello's successful concealment from himself of the knowledge that she couldn't conceivably have been unfaithful to him. See Stanley Cavell, *Disowning Knowledge in Seven Plays of Shakespeare* (Cambridge: Cambridge University Press, 1987), chap. 3.

31. Whether Judas was a "real" traitor or simply acting the part of one in a foundation story is discussed in William Klassen, *Judas: Betrayer or Friend of Jesus?* (London: SCM Press, 1996).

32. See Leonard W. Levy, *Treason Against God: A History of the Offense of Blasphemy* (New York: Schocken Books), 1981.

33. Pierre Manent, *A World Beyond Politics? A Defense of the Nation State* (Princeton, N.J.: Princeton University Press, 2006), 14.

34. During the French Revolution the term "surveillance" for what is today a major arm of the state had the sense of a complementary form of sovereignty as an expression of the "general will." Of course, "sovereignty," like other major concepts of politics, law, and morality, is ambiguous, and therefore contestable and contested.

35. Cited in John Dower, *The Violent American Century* (Chicago: Haymarket Books, 2017), 60.

36. David Trotter, *Paranoid Modernism: Literary Experiment, Psychosis, and the Professionalization of English Society* (Oxford: Oxford University Press, 2001), 77.
37. Trotter, 82–83.
38. Per Klein and La Volpe,

> Secularization is a defining trait of modernity and this secularization is built, in part, on the critique of enthusiasm.... There was an obvious shift in the discourse of anti-enthusiasm from theological polemic to new languages of science and medicine. Perhaps more interesting, however, are the underlying continuities and structural affinities ... between sacred and secular discourses. Most striking is the migration of the discourse of enthusiasm from the domain of religious polemic to the recognizably modern political contestation of the later eighteenth century, especially in the 1790s.... The discourse of enthusiasm was appropriated by both radicals and anti-radicals.

Klein and La Volpe, *Enthusiasm and Enlightenment in Europe*, 4.
39. Michael Wood, "At the Movies: *The Lodger*, directed by Alfred Hitchcock," *London Review of Books* 34, no. 16 (August 30, 2012), https://www.lrb.co.uk/v34/n16/michael-wood/at-the-movies.
40. On this, Dower writes,

> The postwar American leviathan was, and has remained to the present day, essentially bipolar—hubristic and overwhelmingly powerful by all material measures, yet fearful and insecure.... This was, as military planners saw it, less a handicap than a paradox to be exploited. Fear of ominous existential enemies primed the political pump to maintain support for a massive military machine. Anxiety maintained at high levels was a control mechanism that kept politicians and the public in line.... Careers hinged on this. So did the many public and private entities invested in "security." So did "defense"-related industrial profits.

Dower, *The Violent American Century*, 25–26.

41. Every revolutionary state promotes paranoia. Geoffrey Hoskins describes the consequences of the deliberate destruction of everyday routines and publicly recognized reputations in the Russian revolution. "In this milieu," he writes, "everyone became fearful, and learnt to be more distrustful, a tendency which prepared the way for the grotesque levels of distrust prevalent in the 1930s." Geoffrey Hoskins, *Trust: A History* (Oxford: Oxford University Press, 2014), 13. However, political revolution is not the only situation that encourages this outcome: the rapid social change we call modern progress also promotes paranoia. And that in turn is accompanied by and justifies the use of violence and deception by the progressive state.

42. Bernard Harcourt, *Against Prediction: Profiling, Policing, and Punishing in an Actuarial Age* (Chicago: University of Chicago Press, 2007), 2.

43. Ian Hacking, "The Looping Effects of Human Kinds," in *Causal Cognition: A Multidisciplinary Debate*, ed. Dan Sperber, David Premack, and Ann J. Premack (Oxford: Clarendon Press, 1995).

44. See Josef Ansorge, *Identify and Sort: How Digital Power Changed World Politics* (London: C. Hurst & Co., 2016).

45. Pierre Rosanvallon, *The New Social Question: Rethinking the Welfare State* (Princeton, N.J.: Princeton University Press, 2000), 12.

46. Cited in V. P. Bynack, "Noah Webster's Linguistic Thought and the Idea of an American National Culture," *Journal of the History of Ideas* 45, no. 1 (January–March 1984): 99–114, at 99.

47. Bynack, 100.

48. Rosanvallon, *New Social Question*, 21.

49. Ivan Ascher notes that, by the winter of 2007–8,

> it was the entire fabric of society that had been transformed: a third of all profits in the United States were occurring in the financial sector, levels of public and private debt had reached record highs, and access to financial markets—once the privilege of an elite few—had officially become democratized. Commercial banks could now invest with abandon in

the world's financial markets (the Glass-Steagall Act of 1933 having just been repealed), an even greater share of people's retirement savings were being managed by a handful of pension funds (their future, therefore, placed at the mercy of the market's fluctuations), and the U.S. government itself was actively fostering an 'ownership society' in which everyone from Wall Street to Main Street would have some skin in the game.

Ivan Ascher, *Portfolio Society: On the Capitalist Mode of Prediction* (New York: Zone Books, 2016), 13.

50. To this day, insurance remains banned in many Muslim countries—on the grounds of the Qur'anic condemnation of gambling (*maysir*). A more general principle behind the prohibition against financial speculation/gambling is that money is not to be regarded as a commodity, something one can buy and sell for gain. And speculation is forbidden because it is one thing to recognize that there is much one doesn't or can't know ("only God knows") and another to pretend, through betting, that one does and profit accordingly. The Arabic term for insurance in the modern sense, especially insurance provided by for-profit companies (*ta'min*, from *amn*, "security") is, incidentally, displacing another term, *takāful* (from *kafāla*, "guarantee,"), which has the sense of mutual liability or responsibility. The word "*takāful*" is used in that context too, as an arrangement that avoids speculation in financial matters, thus paralleling the organizational experience of working-class "Friendly Societies" in industrializing Europe.

51. Lorraine Daston, *Classical Probability in the Enlightenment* (Princeton, N.J.: Princeton University Press, 1988), 6. Both these features are recognized in the history of the shari'a (in the idea of weak and strong faith, and of equity in aleatory contracts) although their mathematization was not developed in Muslim societies.

52. P. H. J. H. Gosden, *The Friendly Societies in England, 1815–1875* (Manchester, U.K.: Manchester University Press, 1961), 10.

53. John Macnicol, *The Politics of Retirement in Britain, 1878–1948* (Cambridge: Cambridge University Press, 1998), 112.
54. Robin Blackburn has connected the emergence of pensions with suspicion of the elderly during the nineteenth-century revivalist movements. See his interesting *Banking on Death: Or, Investing in Life; the History and Future of Pensions* (London: Verso, 2002).
55. John Macnicol writes that

> in the eighty years after Rose's Act [in 1793] the friendly societies lived an uneasy existence. Like the craft unions, they occupied a twilight world of semi-illegality. (The frequency with which the word "loyal" appeared in their titles was tribute to this, as was the fact that overt political discussion in their meetings was often prohibited.) . . . In short, the societies were inherently weak; and with a politically docile labour aristocracy as members, the state had little need to exercise overt control.

> Macnicol, *Politics of Retirement in Britain*, 114.

56. Macnicol, 113.
57. Gosden cites a speech by the postmaster general in 1880 that responds to the problems encountered by friendly societies in England:

> It cannot, I venture to say, be too constantly borne in mind that self-help and self-reliance are the only sure guarantees for social, national, and, may I add, moral progress. Legislation which encourages the people rather to rest upon State-help than to rely upon themselves, however well-intentioned, will prove *incalculably mischievous* in the end; and to every measure that is brought forward with the object of improving the condition of the people, this simple test should be applied—will it encourage them to rely upon self-help?

> Gosden, *The Friendly Societies in England*, 164, italics supplied. Increasing reliance on for-profit insurance companies was, of course, seen as a part of self-reliance, even although this was eventually a requirement of state legislation.

58. Gosden cites the conclusion of a report by the Board of Agriculture in 1793 as typical of entrenched class suspicion toward them:

> that benefit clubs, holden at public houses, increase the number of those houses, and naturally lead to idleness and intemperance; that they afford commodious opportunities to foment sedition, and form illegal combinations, which they have sometimes actually done; and that as far as I have read and observed, there is not the slightest probability in their general extensive application, that they ever have, or ever will diminish our poor rates but just the contrary....

Gosden, 3.

59. Nob Doran, "Risky Business: Codifying Embodied Experience in the Manchester Unity of Oddfellows," *Journal of Historical Sociology* 7, no. 2 (June 1994): 131–54.

60. As Rosanvallon points out, insurance is the science of spreading risks over a given population and therefore a way of constructing social solidarity. It also has profound implications for the construction of responsibility. But over the last few decades, important changes have occurred in the way risk and responsibility are constructed in Euro-America. In the United States, what historians call the New Deal era—including the postwar institution of Medicare, Medicaid, and natural disaster insurance—public and private insurance expanded significantly, helping to build the much more limited American version of what in Britain came to be known as the welfare state. In Western Europe, the direct experience of war pushed in the same direction. However, with the adoption of neoliberal policies by American and European states, there has been an increasing shift to the privatization of insurance, based partly on the economic argument that individualizing risk would lead to lower claims on collective resources and partly on the moralistic argument that individualizing responsibility was good for character.

61. Perhaps most remarkable is the popular criticism of the death and injury, however minimal, sustained in military action—to American soldiers not to foreign civilians.

62. Shona Brown and Kathleen Eisenhardt, *Competing on the Edge: Strategy as Structured Chaos* (Boston: Harvard Business School Press, 1998); and T. Baker and J. Simon, eds., *Embracing Risk: The Changing Culture of Insurance and Responsibility* (Chicago: University of Chicago Press, 2002).

63. If time is to be defined as the asymmetry of (successive) events, as Ilya Prigogine says, then broken time is the irreparable break between events. See Ilya Prigogine, *The End of Certainty: Time, Chaos, and The New Laws of Nature* (New York: Free Press, 1997).

64. Ironically, the increase of anxiety about terrorist attacks (and the consequent expectation that the state will do everything in its power to protect citizens against them) seems to be accompanied by a growing cultivation of danger as an individual experience—in the form of extreme sports, drug use, and financial speculation.

65. Y. Yamanouchi, J. V. Koschmann, and R. Narita, eds., *Total War and "Modernization"* (Ithaca, N.Y.: Cornell University East Asia Program, 1998).

66. I tried to address this problem in a preliminary way through the early conceptualization of statistics in anthropology—see Talal Asad, "Ethnographic Representation, Statistics and Modern Power," *Social Research* 61, no. 1 (Spring 1994): 55–88. A powerful attack on the negative implications of statistics for democracy by someone who has active experience in the uses of statistics in Wall Street is Cathy O'Neill, *Weapons of Math Destruction* (New York: Crown, 2016).

67. Martijn Konings explains:

> In derivatives markets (typically depicted as the quintessential expression of casino capitalism), any hard-and-fast distinction between hedging and speculative financing breaks down. Risk avoidance and security become themselves speculative propositions, requiring the continuous differentiation of financial positions. Derivatives trading can be understood as responding to the absence of fundamental values (by making risk

itself a tradable commodity) and so can be seen as constituting a (paradoxical) regime of measure.

Martijn Konings, "State of Speculation: Contingency, Measure, and
the Politics of Plastic Value," *South Atlantic Quarterly* 114, no. 2 (2015):
n1.

68. Konings, 273–74.
69. For a discussion of ethnic cleansing in the twentieth century, see
    Michael Mann, *The Dark Side of Democracy: Explaining Ethnic Cleansing*
    (Cambridge: Cambridge University Press, 2005).
70. Jonathan Freedland, "Yearning for the Same Land," *New Statesman*,
    July 18, 2012.
71. Amnon Raz-Krokotzkin, "Secularism, the Christian Ambivalence
    Toward the Jews, and the Notion of Exile," in *Secularism in Question:
    Jews and Judaism in Modern Times*, ed. Ari Joskowitcz and Ethan B. Katz,
    276–98 (University of Pennsylvania Press, 2015), 288.
72. Freedland, "Yearning for the Same Land."
73. The most thorough and reliable account of the ethnic cleansing of
    Palestinians is the Israeli historian Ilan Pappé's *The Ethnic Cleansing of
    Palestine* (Oxford Oneworld, 2007). The United Nations (at that
    time dominated by the Western Powers) accepted the new State of
    Israel as a member without insisting on the return of the Palestinian
    refugees expelled from their homes, an obligation under international
    law that the State of Israel has never fulfilled.
74. "The League's slow collapse in the late 1930s did not signal the end
    of the idea that refugee issues provided a uniquely convincing ratio-
    nale for new forms of international authority," writes the historian
    Laura Robson.

> In 1948, following the British abandonment of the Palestine
> Mandate and the subsequent Zionist expulsion of three-
> quarters of a million Palestinian Arabs, the new UN revived
> this concept of a refugee crisis requiring internationalist
> intervention. The UN's early attempt to find a solution, the
> United Nations Conciliation Commission for Palestine, failed
> in its efforts to press for refugee return and/or compensation;

its successor [the United Nations Relief and Works Agency for
Palestinian Refugees] would have rather different goals, both
more and less ambitious.

Less ambitious in being told to steer clear of the sensitive issue of the
return and/or compensation of the refugees, and more ambitious in
concerning itself with the issue of the economic and social development of a colonial population. Laura Robson, "Refugees and the Case
for International Authority in the Middle East: The League of
Nations and the United Nations Relief and Works Agency for Palestinian Refugees in the Near East Compared," *International Journal of
Middle East Studies* 49, no. 4 (2017): 625–44, at 626.

75. Carl Schmitt, *The Crisis of Parliamentary Democracy* (Cambridge Mass.:
MIT Press, 1988), 10.

76. Interview by Justine Lacroix, "An Interview with Michael Walzer,"
Revue internationale de philosophie 2015/4, no. 274: 459–60, emphasis
added.

77. Lacroix, 459–60.

78. Ernest Renan, "What Is a Nation?" reprinted in Shlomo Sand, *On
the Nation and the 'Jewish People'* (London: Verso, 2010), 45–46.

79. Renan, 64.

80. See, for example, Jean-Pierre Filiu, *From Deep State to Islamic State*
(New York: Oxford University Press, 2015). As is evident from
the book's title, Filiu deals with the contemporary instability and
violence in the Middle East, which he attributes to the deep states
in the region. However, this account does not address the complex
history of Euro-American interventions there (economic, political, and military), nor does it recognize the existence of the deep
state in modern liberal countries.

81. Not only is the consequence of this project for Palestinians in 1947–
48 taken to be now so much water under the bridge, it is in any case
felt to be outweighed by the much greater suffering of the Jewish
people in the past as well as by their religiously based right as a nation
to Palestine—although the leaders of the movement were not themselves religious. However, two interconnected facts are glossed over

in Freedland's attempted justification. First, the Zionist project of acquiring Palestine long predated the Nazi genocide of Jews: a nineteenth-century nationalist movement led by secular Europeans basing their claim to Palestine on the Hebrew Bible (a territory controlled after World War I by the British who decided to concede the Zionist claim to Palestine) has made for a productive ambiguity. Second, whatever the trauma of the Holocaust, the establishment of the State of Israel, together with the ethnic cleansing of Palestinians by Zionist fighters, occurred *after* the threat of destruction directed at European Jewry was over, *after* Nazi power was eliminated. Once that project, in all its secular/religious ambiguity, is accorded supreme moral authority, liberals find it easy to deplore Israeli settlements in the Occupied West Bank as well as the military Occupation itself, but difficult to do anything about them.

82. The claim by nonreligious Jews in the Diaspora to a single culture is discussed in Jakob J. Petuchowski's *Zion Reconsidered* (New York: Twayne Publishers, 1966). This relatively early work by a Jewish theologian considers critically the problem of defining a "Jewish nation." A more recent critique of the familiar ideological history of "the Jewish nation" is Shlomo Sand, *The Invention of the Jewish People* (London: Verso, 2009).

83. This has been interestingly discussed by Raz-Krakotzkin, "Secularism, the Christian Ambivalence Toward the Jews."

84. George Packer, "The Holder of Secrets: Laura Poitras's Closeup View of Edward Snowden," *New Yorker*, October 20, 2014.

85. See Mark Neocleous, *War Power, Police Power* (Edinburgh: University of Edinburgh Press, 2014).

86. Hence, a crucial part of the construction of citizen rights has been the definition of aliens whether transient or living in the national territory on sufferance. After World War II, European states encountered a considerable shortage of labor for reconstruction and development, so they introduced large numbers of workers from their ex-colonies—joined by immigrants from other poorer countries—thus creating the perception that national identity was being diluted. Immigration even in Europe is not historically new, of course—just as

refugees fleeing from war, persecution, and immiseration are not a new phenomenon. What is new is the sudden arrival of numbers of Muslim refugees as European and American states try to rearticulate "social solidarity" in neoliberalism's broken time.

87. Robert Skidelsky, "European Politics with an Islamic Face?" *Project Syndicate*, December 28, 2015, https://www.project-syndicate.org/columnist/robert-skidelsky#Yk6PzkXhhQqhjdYt.99.

88. This sentiment is not new, of course. Pankaj Mishra reminds us that there is a history of British liberals expressing the fear that their "homogeneous culture" would be destroyed by foreigners: "In 1968, Powell warned that immigration from Britain's former colonies would lead to a dire situation in which 'the black man will have the whip hand over the white man;' ten years later, the prime minister-in-waiting Margaret Thatcher claimed in a television interview that British people were 'really rather afraid that this country might be rather swamped by people with a different culture.'" Pankaj Mishra, "What Is Great about Ourselves," *London Review of Books*, vol. 39 no. 18 (September 21, 2017). The idea that a workingman in Yorkshire has the same culture as an upper-class professional family there is quite a remarkable assumption.

89. This has resulted in the modern "purification" of national inhabitants as essentially non-European; the most notorious example is the Nazi genocide of the Jews—and Roma—in the twentieth century. The Turkish genocide of Armenians is coming to be recognized, but there is also an earlier (and less well-known) example: the expulsion of Ottoman Muslims from Eastern Europe. See Justin McCarthy, *Death and Exile: The Ethnic Cleansing of Ottoman Muslims, 1821–1922* (Princeton, N.J.: Darwin Press, 1995).

90. Referring to the demand for state universality that emerged after the French Revolution, Michel Foucault observes:

> The demand will no longer be articulated in the name of a past right that was established by either a consensus, a victory, or an invasion. The demand can now be in terms of a potentiality, a

future, a future that is immediate, which is already present in the present because it concerns a certain function of Statist universality that is already fulfilled by "a" nation within the social body, and which is therefore demanding that its status as a single nation must be effectively recognized, and recognized in the juridical form of the State.

Michel Foucault, *Society Must Be Defended* (New York: Picador, 2003), 222.

91. The equality of those who legitimately belong to the nation-state is at once identified and constructed partly through mathematical criteria. Thus, with reference to the problem of equality I explored in my first chapter, I now suggest that "equality" *can* avoid the charge of being normatively tautological when it is shown to be the result of a practice as opposed to the statement of a general rule—and when this is done through statistics, a language that deals centrally with the construction of equivalences.

92. On "cyborg citizens," see James Hughes, *Citizen Cyborg: Why Democratic Societies Must Respond to the Redesigned Human of the Future* (Cambridge, Mass.: Westview, 2004). For two recent celebrations, see Juan Enriquez and Steve Gullans, *Evolving Ourselves: How Unnatural Selection and Nonrandom Mutation Are Changing Life on Earth* (New York: Penguin, 2016); and Jennifer A. Doudna and Samuel H. Sternberg, *A Crack in Creation: Gene Editing and the Unthinkable Power to Control Evolution* (New York: Houghton Mifflin Harcourt, 2017).

93. Hughes, *Citizen Cyborg*, xii.

94. Hughes, viii.

95. Hughes, 8.

96. One aspect of this power is biohacking:

When biologists synthesize DNA, they take pains not to create or spread a dangerous stretch of genetic code that could be used to create a toxin or, worse, an infectious disease. But one group of biohackers has demonstrated how DNA can carry a less expected threat—one designed to infect not humans nor animals but computers. In new research they plan to present at the USENIX Security conference on Thursday, a group of researchers from the University of Washington has shown for the first time that it is possible to encode malicious software into physical strands of DNA, so that when a gene sequencer analyzes it the resulting data becomes a program that corrupts gene-sequencing software and takes control of the underlying computer. While that attack is far from practical for any real spy or criminal, it's one the researchers argue could become more likely over time, as DNA sequencing becomes more commonplace, powerful, and performed by third-party services on sensitive computer systems. And, perhaps more to the point for the cybersecurity community, it also represents an impressive, sci-fi feat of sheer hacker ingenuity.

Andy Greenberg, "Biohackers Encoded Malware in a Strand of DNA," *Wired*, August 10, 2017. I am grateful to Hussein Agrama, who has been exploring the topic of artificial intelligence, for alerting me to this reference.

97. Abou Farman pursues this paradox in his remarkable study of the beliefs and practices of the cryonics movement. See Abou Ali Farman Farmaian, "Secular Immortal" (PhD diss., Anthropology Department, CUNY Graduate Center, New York, 2012).

Epilogue

1. Sherman Jackson has argued persuasively for a concept of "the Islamic secular," a domain of action and thought outside the shari'a that is nevertheless intrinsic to Islamic tradition. See Sherman Jackson, "The Islamic Secular," in *American Journal of Islamic Social Sciences* 34, no. 2 (Spring 2017): 1–31.

2. For a highly original study that problematizes our understanding of Christianity as a "religion," see Gil Anidjar, *Blood: A Critique of Christianity* (New York: Columbia University Press, 2014).

3. Incidentally, the shift from "religious" to "secular" that Kirstie McClure finds in Locke is also central to the story told by John Dunn about the later rise of political economy. Kirstie McClure, "Taking Liberties in Foucault's Triangle: Sovereignty, Discipline, Governmentality, and the Subject of Rights," in *Identities, Politics, and Rights*, ed. by A. Sarat and T. R. Kearns, 149–92 (Ann Arbor: University of Michigan Press, 1995); and John Dunn, "From Applied Theology to Social Analysis: The Break Between John Locke and the Scottish Enlightenment," in *Wealth and Virtue; The Shaping of Political Economy in the Scottish Enlightenment*, ed. I. Hont and M. Ignatieff, 119–36 (New York: Columbia University Press, 1983). However, there is a complication that Dunn's account ignores: that a reformulated concept of "providence" played a crucial part in the rise of political economy. See M. L. Myers, *The Soul of Modern Economic Man: Ideas of Self-Interest from Thomas Hobbes to Adam Smith* (Chicago: University of Chicago Press, 1983).

4. Herbert Morris, *Guilt and Innocence: Essays in Legal Philosophy and Moral Psychology* (Berkeley: University of California Press, 1976), 151.

5. For a fascinating recent study, see Daniel Morgan, *Astral Science in Early Imperial China: Observation, Sagehood, and the Individual* (Cambridge: Cambridge University Press, 2017).

6. On the "first strike" option, see Sam Knight, "Obama to Stick with 'First Strike' Nuclear War Doctrine, Claiming Deterrence Value," *District Sentinel* September 6, 2016, https://www.districtsentinel.com /obama-stick-first-strike-nuclear-war-doctrine-claiming-deterrence -value/.

7. David Ferry, *Gilgamesh: A New Rendering in English Verse* (New York: Farrar, Straus and Giroux, 1992), 64.

8. Abou Farman, "Terminality," *Social Text* 35, no. 2 (June 2017).

9. Cited in John Dower, *The Violent American Century: War and Terror Since World War II* (Chicago: Haymarket Books, 2017), p. 38.

10. For details and sources on recent developments, see Michael T. Klare, "The Trump Doctrine: Making Nuclear Weapons Usable Again," *Tom Dispatch*, November 19, 2017. http://www.tomdispatch.com/post

/176353/tomgram%3A_michael_klare%2C_normalizing_nukes /#more.

11. Denise Breitburg, Lisa A. Levin, Andreas Oschlies, Marilaure Grégoire, Francisco P. Chavez, Daniel J. Conley, Véronique Garçon, et al., "Declining Oxygen in the Global Ocean and Coastal Waters," *Science* 359, no. 6371 (January 5, 2018).

12. Alasdair MacIntyre once enumerated four systematic sources of unpredictability: (1) radical conceptual innovation, (2) infinitely recurring disjunctions between the unpredictability of one's own action and its predictability by an observer—whose very action as predictor of another is also her own action and therefore unpredictable to herself, (3) the game-theoretic character of social life, and (4) pure contingency. See Alasdair MacIntyre, *After Virtue: A Study in Moral Theory* (Notre Dame, Ind.: University of Notre Dame Press, 1980), 89–95. See also Daniel Boorstin, *Cleopatra's Nose: Essays on the Unexpected* (New York: Random House, 1994).

13. Gramsci was describing his own predicament in a letter from prison: "I'm a pessimist because of intelligence, but an optimist because of will." Unlike the familiar slogan, this sentence does not reify intelligence and will.

14. See, for example, Olivier Roy, *The Failure of Political Islam* (Cambridge, Mass.: Harvard University Press, 1994); and Ami Ayalon, "From Fitna to Thawra," *Studia Islamica* 66 (1987): 145–74.

15. "For all that *is* in the world, the lust of the flesh, and the lust of the eyes, and the pride of life, is not of the Father, but is of the world." 1 John 2:16 (King James Version).

16. David Scott, "Preface: Evil Beyond Repair," *small axe* 55 (March 2018).

17. A typical example of this confidence is this statement from a book I read with great excitement in 1959: "Possibly not all scientists share Peirce's conception of Nature as 'something great, and beautiful, and sacred, and eternal and real—the object of worship and aspiration'; but all must share his faith that there is one real answer to every definite question, that is to say, one answer which is destined to be reached if only the scientific method is pursued far enough." W. B.

Gallie, *Peirce and Pragmatism* (Harmondsworth, Middlesex, U.K.: Penguin, 1952), 92.

18. According to the etymology supplied by Benveniste, "superstition" comes from the root that means "surviving." Emile Benveniste, *Indo-European Language and Society* (London: Faber and Faber, 1973). Initially, therefore, there was nothing pejorative about the word, but when theologians used it to refer to pagan beliefs and practices persisting in a Christianized population, it acquired a sense at once historical and value-laden. In her interesting article "Superstition and Popular Religion in Societies," Belmont states that Victorian anthropologists cleared the notion of its theological overtones by translating it as "survival." Nicole Belmont, "Superstition and Popular Religion in Societies," in *Between Belief and Transgression: Structuralist Essays in Religion, History, and Myth*, ed. M. Izard and P. Smith, 9–23 (Chicago: University of Chicago Press, 1982). But the concept of beliefs and practices that have outlived their proper time is itself a product of transcendental judgment essential to the idea of progress. And when Tylor writes that "the term superstition now implies a reproach, and . . . this reproach may be often cast deservedly on fragments of a dead lower culture embedded in a living higher one," he affirms the theological basis of such judgments; he doesn't deny it. Edward B. Tylor, *Primitive Culture*, vol. 1 (1871; English repr. ed., Gloucester, Mass.: Peter Smith, 1970), 72.

19. A text that employs this old binary (and from which the quotations are taken) is Ali Mirsepassi, *Political Islam, Iran and the Enlightenment: Philosophies of Hope and Despair* (Cambridge: Cambridge University Press, 2011). In the latter, Mirsepassi includes both Islamist and secularist (Marxist and Romantic) movements. A far more sophisticated and thought-provoking book than Mirsepassi's that overlaps with the latter's central concern (but approaches it from a different direction) is Behrooz Ghamari-Tabari, *Foucault in Iran: Islamic Revolution after the Enlightenment* (Minneapolis: University of Minnesota Press, 2016).

20. Hannah Arendt, *The Origins of Totalitarianism*, 2nd ed. (New York: Harcourt Brace & World, 1968), 460. The final chapter was

originally published as an article entitled "Ideology and Terror: A Novel Form of Government," in *Review of Politics* 15, no. 3 (1953): 303–27.

21. Arendt, *Origins of Totalitarianism*, 460. Arendt continues:

> What prepares men for totalitarian domination in the non-totalitarian world is the fact that loneliness, once a borderline experience usually suffered in certain marginal conditions like old age, has become an everyday experience of the evergrowing masses of our century. . . . By destroying all space between men and pressing men against each other, even the productive potentialities of isolation are annihilated; by teaching and glorifying the logical reasoning of loneliness where man knows that he will be utterly lost if ever he lets go of the first premise from which the whole process is being started, even the slim chances that loneliness may be transformed into solitude and logic into thought are obliterated. If this practice is compared with that of tyranny, it seems as if a way had been found to set the desert itself in motion, to let loose a sand storm that could cover all parts of the inhabited earth. The conditions under which we exist today in the field of politics are indeed threatened by these devastating sand storms. Their danger is not that they might establish a permanent world. Totalitarian domination, like tyranny, bears the seeds of its own destruction. Just as fear and the impotence from which fear springs are antipolitical principles and throw men into a situation contrary to political action, so loneliness and the logical-ideological deducing the worst that comes from it represent an anti-social situation and harbor a principle destructive for all human living-together. Nevertheless organized loneliness is considerably more dangerous than the unorganized impotence of all those who are ruled by the tyrannical and arbitrary will of a single man. Its danger is that it threatens to ravage the world as we know it—a world which everywhere seems to have come to an

end—before a new beginning rising from this end has time to assert itself.

Arendt, 478.

22. I have discussed the Islamic tradition of *amr bi-l-ma'ruf* in Talal Asad, "Thinking About Tradition, Religion, and Politics in Egypt Today," *Critical Inquiry* 42 (Autumn 2015) as well as in the last chapter of *Genealogies of Religion: Discipline and Reasons of Power in Christianity and Islam* (Baltimore: Johns Hopkins University Press, 1993), where I give an ethnographic account of the partly overlapping notion of *nasiha*.

23. The conflict between friendship and the nation-state (often benignly called "country") has often been written about. Thus, in a famous comment E. M. Forster wrote, "I hate the idea of causes but if I had to choose between betraying my country and betraying my friend, I hope I should have the guts to betray my country." E. M. Forster, *Two Cheers for Democracy* (London: Edward Arnold, 1951), 66. This remark of Forster's has been denounced by advocates of patriotism, for example:

> Apart from its ignorance and its flair for rationalizing disreputable behavior, the comment depends on a pair of unproven assumptions: that there is always a gulf between people and principle, and that it is better to betray a good principle than a bad person. Forster may have recognized the precariousness of these assumptions if he had been an American, because ours is the only country in the world founded solely on ideas. . . . To renounce betrayal of country is to embrace our land, affirm the principles in our founding documents, and extend a vote of confidence to our fellow citizens.

Patrick O'Hannigan, "E. M. Forster and the Politics of Btrayal," https://www.billstclair.com/lodge/F_PoliticsOfBetrayal.shtml. What for Forster was an agonizing conflict between the bond of mutual dependence and love between friends (that can be profoundly damaged but not totally eliminated by betrayal) and the principle of unconditional commitment to the power of the nation-state (that carries a serious legal penalty if it is violated) is here presented glibly as "rationalizing disreputable behavior."

24. The full sentence, cited in the canonical *hadīth* collection Sahih Muslim, reads as follows: *"man rā'a minkum munkaran fa-la-ghayyarahu bi-yadihi; fa in lam yastati' fa-bi-lisānihi; fa in lam yastati' fa-bi-qalbihi; wa dhālik ad'af-ul-imān."*

25. In a fascinating book, Emily Ogden has recently traced the ambiguous history of "mesmerism" (overlapping in part with the more familiar "hypnotism") as an Enlightenment understanding of the origins of superstitious belief in magic and the occult—but also of using that understanding to impart rationalist truth in such domains as modern education, psychological healing, and the regulation of labor. See Emily Ogden, *Credulity: A Cultural History of Mesmerism* (Chicago: University of Chicago Press, 2018).

26. The role of theoretically inspired suggestibility is evident in a beautifully written book, *Tribute to Freud,* by an American patient and admirer who signs herself H.D.

INDEX

artificial intelligence, 144
Ascher, Ivan, 189n49
Ascherson, Neal, 33
Augustine, St., 75
Austin, J. L., 64, 183n8
authenticity, 91–92
authoritarianism, 45
authority, 39, 183n7
awe of God (*birr wa taqwa*), 76

behavior, 68
behavioral customs (*'urf 'amali*), 95
belief, spontaneity and, 91
Belmont, Nicole, 201n18
benefit clubs, 191n58
Benjamin, Walter, 8–9, 51, 148
bias, equality of opportunity and, 26–27
bi-nnafsi-l-lawwāmati (blaming or criticizing soul), 73
biohacking, 197–98n96
bioLuddites, 145
biopolitics, as state role, 126
birr wa taqwa (awe of God), 76
Black Lives Matter, 27–28
blaming or criticizing soul (*bi-nnafsi-l-lawwāmati*), 73
blasphemy, 113–14, 116
Bloch, Maurice, 102–3, 172n9
Blumenberg, Hans, 15–16
Board of Agriculture (England), 191n58
bodies: in action, language of, 45; body-mind duality, 90; indigenous conceptions of,

175n20; life as information versus embodied life, 144–45; prayer as embodied practice, 86–87; Qur'an, bodily incorporation of, 65–66, 175n19; sensible body, 61–62, 64–65, 103; of women, 52. *See also* translation, sensible body and
boycotts, 160
Branch, Lori, 90–91
Brentano, Franz, 79
Britain. *See* England, Britain and United Kingdom
Buddhism, Habermas on, 50
Butler, Lee, 153

Cairo, Egypt, piety movement in, 54
calculation. *See* numbers, language of
Calvinism, 166–67n20
capitalism, risk and, 134
care of the self, 74–75, 110
Cartesian psychology, 85–86
"A Category of the Human Mind" (Mauss), 100
Cavell, Stanley, 186n30
certainty, desire for, 116, 117, 120
charity tax, Islamic, 179–80n52
Christianity: Christian metaphysics, in Britain, 41–42; Christians, nature of lives of, 74; cultural pluralism of, 56; as historical origin of secularism,

GPSR Authorized Representative: Easy Access System Europe, Mustamäe tee
50, 10621 Tallinn, Estonia, gpsr.requests@easproject.com